D0393790

More Praise for

The Happiness of Pursuit

"When a quest is a journey or a sought-after goal, it can be satisfying, fun, even paradigm shifting. But when a quest begins with an inner yearning and transforms into a calling, it becomes medicine for the soul, and this changes *everything*. **The Happiness of Pursuit is an invitation to listen to the part of oneself that craves purpose. It says, 'Hey! Wake up! Your unique adventure awaits you.'**"

—LISSA RANKIN, M.D., *New York Times* bestselling author of *Mind Over Medicine*

"The incredible quests Chris Guillebeau explores in *The Happiness of Pursuit,* including his own to visit every country, left me feeling exhausted. Of course, as a person who works from home, I limit my quests most days to taking a shower. **Bottom line: these stories *are* inspiring—and very, very entertaining.**"

—JOEL STEIN, columnist for *Time* magazine and author of *Man Made: A Stupid Quest for Masculinity*

"Chris Guillebeau doesn't want you to settle for a life that's just a routine. He thinks it should be an adventure. His advice on how to design and achieve your own transformative 'quest' is invaluable—and, even better, his enthusiasm is infectious."

—KEN JENNINGS, record-setting *Jeopardy!* champion and *New York Times* bestselling author of *Maphead*

"Go ahead and admit it: You've got a dream in you, something you want to fulfill, a quest that perhaps you haven't yet shared with anyone. **Chris Guillebeau—who, by the way, has completed his *own* quest of visiting every country in the entire world—has written the book that should be your very first stop**."

—ERIN MCHUGH, author of *One Good Deed: 365 Days of Trying to Be Just a Little Bit Better*

"**Chris Guillebeau is a true Renaissance Man. In *The Happiness of Pursuit* he shows us how the power of a quest can transform lives.** Adventure comes in many forms, but having the courage to pursue one's true calling is what defines a life worth living. Guillebeau inspires readers to do just that, no matter whom they are or where their passions lie. **This is a must-read for anyone seeking that spark of insight that will ignite the inner fire**."

—DEAN KARNAZES, acclaimed endurance athlete and *New York Times* bestselling author

"As someone who walked almost every block in New York City— 121,000 of them—I can really relate to this wonderful book. **Guillebeau's stories of the incredible challenges that people set for themselves and meet are perspective altering and even inspiring.** Most of all, they teach us that life occurs but once and that we can, if we try our hardest, make the most of it."

—WILLIAM HELMREICH, author of *The New York Nobody Knows: Walking 6,000 Miles in the City*

The Happiness of Pursuit

Also by Chris Guillebeau

The $100 Startup

The Art of Non-Conformity

The
Happiness
of Pursuit

Finding the Quest That Will
Bring Purpose to Your Life

Chris Guillebeau

HARMONY
BOOKS · NEW YORK

Library of Congress Cataloging-in-Publication Data
is available upon request.

ISBN 978-0-385-34884-3
eBook ISBN 978-0-385-34885-0

Printed in the United States of America

Book design by Barbara Sturman
Illustration on page 125 by Nicholas Felton
Illustration on page 219 by Mike Rohde
Jacket design by Michael Nagin
Title type: Jessie Sayward Bright
Jacket illustration: Anthonycz/Shutterstock
Author photograph: Stephanie D. Zito

2 4 6 8 10 9 7 5 3 1

First Edition

Contents

I. Beginnings

II. Journey

III. Destination

The Happiness of Pursuit

I.
Beginnings

———

Prologue

On the Road

It was nearly one a.m. when I stepped off a plane and stumbled into the international airport in Dakar, Senegal.

I'd been here many times before, but it always took a moment to regain my bearings. Everywhere I turned, a different guy offered to help with my bags—a series of offers I didn't need, since I always travel light—but the persistent porters were hard to turn down. A shouting match erupted between two of the men. I knew what the stakes were: Whoever served as my escort would be eligible for the tip.

I picked out one of the porters at random and followed him to a small alcove above the shouting crowd. A couple of plastic chairs were nailed to the floor. "Here," he told me in French. "You can stay here and sleep." I looked at the chairs, paid off the guy, and set up camp for what I knew would be a long night.

My final destination was the tiny republic of Guinea-Bissau, just half an hour by air from Dakar, but the flight didn't leave until seven a.m. What to do for six hours?

I could have gone into the city and found a hotel, but the prospect of three hours of sleep before trudging back to the airport wasn't enticing. Better to ride it out until I reached my final destination and was able to crash in a real bed.

I had a bottle of water, procured upon arrival, and a three-ounce bottle of vodka, procured in the Frankfurt airport lounge prior to heading to Africa earlier that day. Together with an airline blanket (thanks, Lufthansa) was all I needed for a few hours of fitful sleep.

Four days earlier I had walked in the rain past Grand Central Terminal in Manhattan. My destination was a tiny consulate office in a sublet United Nations building. The office had no listed hours. For a fee of $100—payable in cash, no receipt provided—I received the visa I'd been hunting down for several months.

This trip would take me from New York to Frankfurt to Dakar to Bissau, and then back out via Lisbon and London a few days later. It was both a journey and a task.

❂

Even when you're worn down from three continents of travel, it's hard to sleep on a plastic chair in a West African transit area. I was careful to keep the strap from my laptop bag coiled around my leg, but still woke with a jolt every few moments as I worried about a return visit from the "helpful" porters. When I managed to drift into real sleep, a swarm of mosquitoes arrived to keep watch, ensuring that I never dozed for long.

I thought about what a laughable experience it was. Why, after having achieved a healthy measure of career success, with plenty of projects at home and a worldwide community of friends in more pleasant surroundings, did I find myself propped up on a plastic chair in the middle of the night in Senegal?

What *was* the journey and the task?

First things first. This area of the world is where it all started, many years ago. Ten years earlier I had roamed the region as an aid worker, serving as a volunteer for a medical charity. Through trial and error I learned how to avoid bribes (well, except for airport porters) and make my way through chaotic arrival scenes like the one I encountered tonight.

So why had I returned?

It was simple, really. This time I was on a different kind of mission. For the past decade I had devoted much of my time, money, and attention to visiting every country in the world. Every single country in every region, with no country left behind—it was a lifelong challenge I had pondered for years before finally accepting it as the quest I would pursue for as long as it took.

This mission had led me to breakaway former Soviet republics and remote islands in the South Pacific. I'd watched the only flight of the night on another small island take off without me. I'd successfully arrived in Pakistan and Saudi Arabia without a visa, somehow convincing the immigration authorities to let me stay. I'd been deported from a country I'm still trying to forget.

Along the way there were many nights like this one in Dakar, where I arrived with no plans except onward travel, flying or riding in a crowded minibus to another small country that made the news only when it was in civil war or threatened with disappearance due to climate change.

In a weird, almost masochistic way, I liked the idea of returning to Senegal. Full circle, back to the beginning, that kind of thing.

After more than 190 countries, the journey would soon be coming to an end. Not yet, though. First I had to make it to Guinea-Bissau, my final country in Africa.

☯

The Dakar airport won't win any awards for overnight stays, but when the sun rises over West Africa, it's worth waking up for. It happens very quickly—shift your eyes and you'll miss it. One minute hazy, the next minute *Rise and shine, traveler!*

By that point I had stumbled back down to the check-in zone and cleared the relaxed security point. I bought an instant coffee and sipped it as I stood in the queue for boarding.

Far from home, there's a feeling you can experience even when you're bone-weary. No matter how exhausted (*Eighteen hours of flying! Two hours of sleep on a plastic chair.*), and no matter how ridiculous the situation (*I'm flying to Guinea-Bissau for no good reason!*), you can still savor the thrill of adventure. As the caffeine kicked in and I stretched my legs, I began to feel better. As crazy as it may have seemed to some people, I was out in the world, doing something I loved. Life was good.

The half-hour flight took us along the coastline at low altitude. The sun fully unfolded in the sky, I dozed against the window seat, and before I knew it we were wheels-down in the capital city.

Landing on the other side, there was no jet bridge that led to a shiny arrivals hall, or even a passenger bus to ferry arrivals to the building. I walked down the stairs of the aging aircraft onto the tarmac and directly into the dusty immigration building a short distance away.

The welcoming committee appeared to have taken the day off. Instead, a lone immigration guy glanced at my papers and stamped me through without a word.

I watched as the bags were thrown onto a single creaky conveyer belt. Once again, the porters fought over rights to luggage duties. The morning with the beautiful sunrise was dissolving into a sweltering day, and another group of men competed to become the chosen taxi driver to deliver the occasional foreigner to the only hotel.

But I smiled at my good fortune, for I had just achieved another milestone on the long quest to go everywhere. Out of fifty-four African countries, Guinea-Bissau was my very last. After ten years of exploration, I had only two more countries to go before completing the whole world.

Once Upon a Time

People have always been captivated by quests. History's earliest stories tell of epic journeys and grand adventures. Whether the history is African, Asian, or European, the plotline is the same: A hero sets off in search of something elusive that has the power to change both their life and the world.

In the Judeo-Christian story of creation, Adam and Eve are banished from the garden of Eden and sent to toil the earth. In the Buddhist story, the question of practice and struggle is emphasized over creation—sacred texts skip straight to the quest toward enlightenment.

The world's best-known literature reflects our desire to hear about struggle and sacrifice in pursuit of a goal. From Aesop's Fables to Arabian Nights, many classic stories are about adventure and quests.

Shakespeare kept us enthralled with quest stories of shipwrecks and mistaken identity. Sometimes all was well that ended well, but sometimes tragedy followed as the natural consequence of a flawed character's poor decisions.

In modern times, Hollywood knows that quests are an easy sell. Consider the blockbuster franchises Star Wars, Star Trek, Indiana Jones, and countless others. The tougher the odds and the higher the stakes, the better—as long as the audience has something to believe in. We have to believe in a hero's mission, and once we do, we'll gladly stick around to see how the hero can overcome.

The best video games, which now draw more of our money and attention than books or movies, are also programmed around quest stories. You, an ordinary soul plucked from obscurity, have been entrusted with defending the earth from an alien invasion. (Conveniently, you have been supplied with a rocket launcher and a rechargeable health pack.) You, a mere plumber with a stubborn disposition and an especially hard head, must rescue the princess from the castle. (Oh, this is the wrong castle? I guess you'll have to keep going.)

Most of these quest stories are told over and over in different ways, often with a fair amount of exaggeration. They can be engaging stories, but for the most part they aren't real. We enjoy them because, for a brief time, they have the power to alter our belief in what's possible. Maybe there really *is* an alien invasion! Maybe there really *is* a holy grail somewhere out there, just waiting to be discovered.

❂

As I wandered the planet, spending years journeying to nearly two hundred countries, I discovered something important.

I loved the travel, and everywhere I went had something interesting on offer. My worldview was broadened as I encountered different ways of life and learned from people in other cultures. But equally fascinating was that I wasn't the *only* one on a quest. All over the world, people had discovered the same way of bringing greater purpose to their life. Some had been toiling away at a goal for years without *any* recognition. Going for it, whatever "it" was, was simply something they found meaningful and loved to do.

"I want to make my life worthwhile," one woman said. "I consider myself an instrument, and if I don't put myself to work for the greatest possible good, I'll feel like I wasted a chance that will never return."

Some of the people I talked to were pursuing quests that involved extended world journeys like mine. I met strangers and new friends who walked, biked, or otherwise traveled across entire countries or continents. In Istanbul, for example, I met Matt Krause, a financial analyst from Seattle. Matt had traveled to Turkey with the intention of walking all the way to Iran, meeting strangers along the way and understanding a different way of life. At first it was just a crazy idea, he said. But then it stuck with him, becoming something he knew he'd regret if he didn't see it through. (Lesson: Beware of crazy ideas.)

Meanwhile, other quests were about mastery or collection. A Boy Scout earned every merit badge (154!) by the age of fifteen. A middle-aged woman devoted the rest of her life to seeing every possible species of bird. As she explained in her journal, what started as a hobby turned into an obsession after receiving a diagnosis of terminal cancer.

Some people's quests were distinctly private. A teenager from the Netherlands set out to sail the open sea, becoming the youngest person in history to successfully circumnavigate the world's oceans alone. The publicity she received from the record-setting adventure was often critical and largely unwelcome. But receiving attention, whether positive or negative, wasn't the point. "I did this for myself," she told me after she'd finished. "Not for anyone else."

Others chose to join forces, including a family of four who set out to bicycle 17,300 miles from Alaska to Argentina, building a dream together along the way. Also feeling wanderlust was a young couple who visited every basilica in the United States hoping to better understand their faith.

Much of the time, the quest was something physical: a mountain to climb, the open sea to traverse, the visa processing office to persuade. But what these strivers were searching for usually went beyond the stated task. Matt Krause, the financial analyst who set out to walk the entire length of rural Turkey, reflected on the life he'd known back in America. It wasn't just that he was now in another country, he said later. It felt as though he'd opened a path to another life. Out there on his own, walking mile after mile along the dusty village roads, meeting strangers who became friends, he felt a heightened sense of being alive.

Something about these people I met stood out. They spoke with intensity. They were focused on their goals, even if they didn't immediately make sense to others. I wanted to understand why they'd chosen to pursue big goals with such determination—were they driven by the same urges as I was or ones that were entirely different?—and I wanted to learn what kept them going when others would have stopped. I had the strong sense that these people could teach critical lessons.

❧

What were the lessons in *my* ten-year journey?

The first lessons were about the practical aspects of pursuing a quest. If you want to achieve the unimaginable, you start by imagining it. Before beginning, take the time to count the cost. Understanding exactly what you need to do, and then finding a way to do it, makes a quest much more feasible.

Courage comes through achievement but also through the attempt. As I worked my way through country after country, regrouping at one of the many stops along the way that felt like second homes, I became more optimistic about my chances of success. In the final year of the journey, I felt unstoppable. *I can really do this!* I realized, and the realization gave me strength and endurance.

As Don Quixote learned many years ago, quests do not always develop as planned. Travelers are often waylaid or misdirected, and some challenges prove especially difficult. Yet misadventures (and sometimes even disasters) produce confidence. When I found myself spending all night in a deserted airline terminal, waiting on another canceled flight, or completely out of money in a remote part of the world, I learned that things would usually be OK. I learned to laugh at my own misfortune, or at least to not panic when something bad happened.

The next lessons were more about the inner work of an extended journey. Many quests lead to an alchemy-like transformation, either with respect to the quest itself or the person undertaking it. Once you start down the road to adventure, you don't always know where you'll end up.

Coming to the end of a quest brings lessons too. The story doesn't always tie up well. When something has been a major part of your life for years and then is gone, a sense of alienation can set in. You have to think about what's next, and whether you can re-create the intense feelings you had during the time you were chasing down your goal.

As my journey neared its end, I wondered what I could learn by talking to others. My curiosity about questing became a quest in itself—one that, it turns out, allows me to offer guidance to those who are themselves engaged in a search for meaning.

Chapter 1

Awakening

It's a dangerous business, Frodo, going out your front door. You step out on to the road, and if you don't keep your feet, there's no knowing where you'll be swept off to. —J. R. R. TOLKIEN

Lesson: ADVENTURE IS FOR EVERYONE.

We live in interesting times, a remarkable age that offers countless opportunities for personal growth and advancement. As busy as we all are, most of us still have enough free time to pursue hobbies and the development of nonessential skills. For the price of a plane ticket, we can jet off to foreign lands. Whatever we could possibly want to learn is readily available to us.

Yet these opportunities can also be overwhelming. After our basic needs are met, how do we choose a focus? For many of us, the answer is surprisingly simple: We choose to embrace a quest, and we choose to live for adventure.

At meetups and coffee shops on five continents, I sought out people who were undertaking quests and heard their stories. Through a series of interviews and surveys, I pestered them about why they chose to focus on a specific goal for an extended period of time. What did they learn, and how were they changed along the way?

Regardless of what kind of project it was, I noticed that people who pursue quests tend to have a few things in common. For example, I talked with a number of people who walked, cycled, or sailed thousands of miles on their own. I didn't want to walk, cycle, or sail thousands of miles (I preferred airplanes). Those who felt compelled to make such journeys probably weren't interested in what I had to deal with either (presumably they didn't want to spend countless nights attempting to sleep on airport floors, or countless days dealing with corrupt officials in stressful situations). But the challenge itself—the ambition of the pursuit and the desire to do whatever it took to keep going—that was the common thread.

In seeking answers, I also borrowed an approach I used in my previous book, *The $100 Startup*. For that project, a small team and I cast a net far and wide, seeking stories from around the globe. One thing led to another and the book's stories seemed to accumulate easily, with one interesting person leading to another.

I faced a greater challenge this time, however. If you're looking for stories of people who've started a business without much money or education, the criteria are clear. But what stories should you search for when it comes to questing?

Working with another small team and a large supply of coffee, I started by once again casting a wide net, this time in search of anyone who'd undertaken a big journey or purposeful adventure. By leaving the initial casting call open-ended, we hoped to hear from a wide variety of diverse subjects. Because people who are pursuing a big quest aren't always online (and because some don't actively speak about their projects), we encouraged readers to submit other people's stories as well.

Having an open casting call was a good starting point, but we quickly realized that we'd need to apply some stricter criteria. Among the initial responses was a broad group of submissions related to general life improvement: getting in shape, for example, or starting a small business, or writing a book. All of these things are fine and well, we thought, but they aren't exactly *quests*. Deciding to improve one's life, however meaningful it might be on a personal level, is not by itself a quest. Quitting smoking, losing weight, or getting out of debt are all worthy pursuits, but they shouldn't be a lifelong focus.

A quest, we decided, is something bigger. It takes more time and requires more commitment than general life improvement. Still, though, what exactly *is* a quest? How to define it?

We decided to let the stories lead the way. Walking across the continent and not speaking for a decade? Yes, that counts. Giving up a well-paying job to advocate for women's rights in Bangladesh . . . as a volunteer with no recognition for twenty years? Yes, that too.

After much consideration, here are the criteria we settled on.

A quest has a clear goal and a specific end point. You can clearly explain a quest in a sentence or two. Every quest has a beginning, and sooner or later, every quest will come to an end. (Not everyone will understand *why* you undertook the quest, but that's another matter.)

A quest presents a clear challenge. By design, a quest requires that something be overcome. Not every quest needs to be dangerous or next to impossible to achieve, but it shouldn't be easy, either.

A quest requires sacrifice of some kind. There is no "having it all" when it comes to a quest—to pursue a big dream, you must give something up along the way. Sometimes the sacrifice is apparent in the beginning; other times it becomes apparent only later on.

A quest is often driven by a calling or sense of mission. A calling need not be some form of divine inspiration. It is often expressed simply as a deep sense of internal purpose. Whatever form it takes, people who pursue quests feel driven, pushed, or otherwise highly motivated to keep going.

A quest requires a series of small steps and incremental progress toward the goal. As we'll see, many quests are composed of a long, slow-and-steady march toward something, with moments of glory and elation few and far between. You don't simply arrive at the holy grail the day after you set out to find it. (If you do, it's probably not the holy grail, and it's definitely not a quest.)

To sum it up, a quest is a journey toward something specific, with a number of challenges throughout. Most quests also require a series of logistical steps *and* some kind of personal growth.

Before anything else can be done, you have to sort out the many practical details and obstacles that lie in your way. In my case I had to arrange visas and methods of transport. I had to figure out how to visit hostile countries that didn't exactly have a tourist department on hand to answer questions or distribute sightseeing brochures. When I ran into problems, I had to retreat and regroup, and then plan for another attempt.

But in a true, life-altering quest, it's not only the practical aspects you have to consider. You also must become a better person than you were before you started. You must improve throughout the journey.

Oh, and there's one more thing I learned: Most of the time, something else happens along the way.

Why a Quest Might Be for You

This book will offer the opportunity to examine dozens of quests, projects, and adventures. If you're already beginning to think about how to apply these lessons and stories to your own life, consider these questions. The more you're inclined to answer "yes," the more likely you are to enjoy a quest of your own.

- Do you like making lists and checking things off?
- Have you always enjoyed setting goals?
- Do you feel motivated by making progress toward a goal?
- Do you enjoy planning?*
- Do you have a hobby or passion that not everyone understands?
- Do you ever find yourself daydreaming or imagining a different kind of life?
- Do you spend a lot of time thinking about your hobby or passion?

---

* Research shows that we enjoy planning a vacation as much as taking the vacation. Anticipation is a powerful force.

A Taxonomy of Adventure

In ancient myths, most quests were ones of discovery or confrontation. A kingdom was under siege, so it required defending. A minotaur in a faraway land guarded a magic chalice, and only the hero could wrest it back.

Happily, real-world quests offer more possibilities than storming castles and rescuing princesses, and with some exceptions modern-day quests can be placed into a few broad categories. Travel is an obvious starting point. As I searched for stories and recruited submissions from readers, I learned of many people who set out to circumnavigate the globe in different fashions or be the first to accomplish a challenging goal far from home.

Branching out beyond travel, the categories of learning, documenting, and athleticism were also fairly self-explanatory. When an independent learner from Canada decided to tackle the four-year MIT computer science curriculum in just one year, publishing his test scores along the way, this was clearly a quest oriented around learning and achievement. When a young woman who competed in international competitions decided to adopt and train an especially difficult horse— eventually placing near the top in an important European championship—this was clearly an athletic pursuit.

Perhaps more interesting than topical categories is the broader question of *why* people pursue quests and adventures. The answers can fit into categories, too, albeit ones that are not as tightly boxed. As I traveled the world and traversed my inbox, a few themes kept coming up:

Self-discovery. Just as heroes of old set off on horses to chase their dreams into enchanted forests, many people still follow paths to "find" themselves. Nate Damm, who walked across America, and Tom Allen, who set out to cycle the planet from his town in England, originally left home merely because they could. They wanted to challenge themselves by learning more about the world. Some of their friends and family understood their desire to set out on big journeys—both gave up jobs to do so—but others didn't get it. "This is just something I need to do," Nate said. "It's about letting a little risk into your life," Tom explained.

Reclaiming. In days of old, reclaiming was about taking back the land. Recall Mel Gibson in his classic *Braveheart* performance standing on a hill and shouting "Freeeee-dooom!" in defense of Scotland against the tyrant Englishmen from the south.

Many people still pursue quests of reclaiming, though not usually with swords and shields. Sasha Martin, a woman raising a family in Oklahoma, had grown up living abroad and wanted to introduce her household to an awareness of different cultures. She couldn't travel to foreign lands, at least not at the time, so she decided to make a meal from every country, complete with an entire menu and mini-celebration.

From the frontiers of Alaska, Howard Weaver led a scrappy team that took on an establishment newspaper. In an epic battle that stretched for years, Howard and his staff fought to present a "voice of the people" against a better-funded, big-business paper.

Response to external events. Sandi Wheaton, a career employee for General Motors, was laid off at the height of the auto industry's downturn in 2009. Instead of choosing the usual strategy (panic, then do everything you can to get another job), she took off for an extended trip, taking photos and documenting the journey as she went along. My own quest to visit every country initially came from a post-9/11 experience, after which I wanted to find a way to meaningfully contribute. My soul-searching led to four years on a hospital ship in West Africa, which sparked everything that would come later.

Desire for ownership and empowerment. Julie Johnson, a blind woman who trained her own guide dog, said that she was motivated at least partly by the pressure put on her *not* to do it her own way. "Probably the biggest reason is that it felt right," she told me. "I needed to do this Big Thing. I didn't know then that it was a Big Thing, I just knew it was something that I needed to do for myself. If I didn't, I'd always wonder about what could have been." This perspective—"If I didn't try, I'd always wonder what might have happened"—showed up again and again in the stories I came across.

Taking a stand for something. Some people I met were essentially missionaries or crusaders for their causes, sharing their stories with anyone who'd listen and building alliances along the way. Miranda Gibson, for example, spent more than a year living in a tree in Tasmania, protesting illegal logging. Others devoted their lives to something they believed in, sacrificing income and time (and sometimes more) to give all that they could.

There's an Adventure Waiting for You, Too

Real-life adventure isn't only about traveling the world (although many of this book's stories do involve travel) nor is a quest always about leaving home (although it often involves breaking out of a comfort zone). Over the next two hundred–plus pages, you'll encounter dozens of incredible stories. You'll meet the people I've mentioned thus far and many more. And you'll learn that the vast majority of these stories are about normal people doing remarkable things.

Sure, there are exceptions: the story of John "Maddog" Wallace comes to mind. Wallace pulled off the feat of running 250 marathons in a single year, ignoring a legion of sports doctors and athletes who all said such a thing was impossible. You may be interested in *why* he did it, or even *how* he did it—but it's not likely you'll try the same thing. That's OK, though. As I've said, most of this book's "cast of characters" are ordinary, in the sense that they don't have special powers or abilities. Their quests—and in many cases, their accomplishments—were extraordinary, but for the most part these individuals were successful not because of innate talent, but because of their choices and dedication.

Much of the time, the goals grew in proportion with time and experience. Those I interviewed often spoke of their perceived feebleness, or of their belief that "anyone" could do what they did—but as you'll see, few would have the resolve to persist as they did.

In addition to satisfying my own curiosity, I wrote this book to inspire you to attempt something remarkable of your own. Look closely here and you'll see a path you can follow, no matter your goal. Everyone who pursues a quest learns many lessons along the way. Some relate to accomplishment, disillusionment, joy, and sacrifice—others to the specific project at hand. But what if you could learn these lessons earlier? What if you could study with others who've invested years— sometimes decades—in the relentless pursuit of their dreams?

That learning opportunity is what this book is about. You'll sit with people who have pursued big adventures and crafted lives of purpose around something they found deeply meaningful. You'll hear their stories and lessons. You'll learn what happened along the way, but more important, you'll learn *why* it happened and why it matters. It's my job as the author to provide a framework and issue a challenge. It's yours to decide the next steps.

Perhaps reading about other people's stories will prompt you to think about your own life. What excites you? What bothers you? If you could do anything at all without regard to time or money, what would it be?

As you progress through this book you'll see that it advances a clear argument: *Quests bring meaning and fulfillment to our lives.* If you've ever wondered if there's more to life, you might discover a world of opportunity and challenge waiting for you. But think of your *first* quest as reading this book. There's a clear goal (finish the book) and a specific end point (the last page). Accomplishing the goal requires time and commitment. Hopefully, the sacrifice won't be huge, but the point is, right now, you could be doing something else instead of reading.

Just Take That First Step

It's hard to put into words the excitement that wells up when you buck routine and begin doing something you were meant to do. I remember my first six-month stop when I volunteered aboard that hospital ship in West Africa. When I glanced out at the sea of faces in Sierra Leone, I felt remarkably alive. Above the dock lay the hills of Freetown, a place of abundant natural beauty marred by the devastation of an eight-year civil war that had only recently ended.

I jumped headfirst into West African life, and along the way learned about travel. The local version was fascinating. Shared taxis crawled through the streets of Freetown, picking up as many as a dozen passengers in a single car. One time I saw a cab swing by and the backseat was empty . . . except for a dead cow, which had somehow been wedged in for transport from one side of the city to another.

Traveling around the region was also interesting. Due to the poorly developed flight network, I often had to make three or more stops in neighboring countries to travel a distance the equivalent of New York to Chicago. The governments of these countries didn't always like one another, so arriving passengers were treated with suspicion, even if they were obviously just passing through en route to their actual destinations.

It was all new and thrilling. I spent my early mornings running on the docks before the sun became too hot. During the day I unloaded medical cargo and coordinated logistics, and at night I sat on the promenade deck to reflect on my surroundings.

By the time the four-year commitment ended, I was eager for a new challenge. I'd been traveling around Africa and

Europe, exploring more and more countries whenever I got the chance. On one trip I flew overnight from Paris to Johannesburg, wide awake and dreaming the whole way, memorizing the Air France route map and considering all the cities I still didn't know.

I wasn't sure how I would do it, but I was entranced by the notion of frequent travel—and I liked the idea of connecting it to a goal. By that point I was busy making lists of the places I wanted to visit. I'd seen a lot, no doubt, but there were far more places I *hadn't* been to.

Even as I began my adventures by living and traveling in a challenging region where tanks patrolled the cities and street lamps were pocked with bullet holes, some parts of travel intimidated me. I wasn't good at speaking other languages, and I didn't feel especially brave. When I looked at the map and considered *the whole world,* I felt overwhelmed. Yet I was oddly attracted to the idea of going everywhere, and something about it reminded me of playing video games.

Ever since I was a kid, I enjoyed gaming. My favorite games were those that involved multiple stages and lots of obstacles to work through. The object of many of these games was to reach the end and emerge victorious, but for me, the game itself was what I enjoyed. Stage by stage, level by level, one triumphant fight after another—I was engaged the most when the game presented challenges that could be overcome through repeated effort and logical thinking.

Something about the gaming concept of *going everywhere* spoke to me. If I made a list and worked on the list, a big goal—even a huge goal—seemed feasible. Country by country, I'd work through the challenge. It wasn't just about the achievement, it was about the effort. I enjoyed the process of tackling the world, going farther and farther afield to places that were largely unfamiliar before I began—if I even knew of them at all. Eventually I'd reach the final stage, but the game itself was what I enjoyed.

Why should *you* consider a quest? Because your life is good, but you don't feel completely fulfilled. You long for a challenge that requires you to develop new muscles and acquire new skills, and if you're willing to work for it, you can find it . . . or perhaps even better, you can create it for yourself.

Remember

A quest has a few key features, including a clear goal, a real challenge, and a set of milestones along the way.

Pay attention to the ideas that draw your interest, especially the ones you can't stop thinking about.

This book isn't just a study of what other people have done. You, too, can identify and pursue a quest.

Chapter 2

The Great Discontent

Discontent is the first necessity of progress.
—THOMAS A. EDISON

Lesson: UNHAPPINESS CAN LEAD TO
NEW BEGINNINGS.

I f you've ever dreamed of escaping to a new life, if you've ever
thought of changing the world, if you've ever said to yourself,
"There must be more to life than this," you're not the only one.

If you've ever felt a strange sense of alienation, a frustration that's hard to pin down, you've known *discontent.* When
discontent sets in, it's time to make some changes. In a world
where so much is possible, yet so many people are unhappy,
there has to be another way.

❂

Five days a week for twelve years, Sandi Wheaton exchanged
the most productive hours of her day for a steady paycheck.
She worked at General Motors headquarters in Detroit, making training broadcasts. As jobs go, it was a good one, and
Sandi was able to spend her free time taking and editing photos, her true passion.

One day she and six of her colleagues were called to an off-site meeting at a nearby hotel, where they were all given the news: "We're sorry and we wish you the best . . . elsewhere." Even though the automotive industry was in crisis, the news came as a shock. Sandi had always prided herself on being responsible and diligent. Approaching midlife, she'd never been out of work before. Sandi was angry, disappointed, and scared.

Her first reaction was to follow the lead of her former colleagues. They had all been laid off on what was termed "Black Friday" among GM employees, and most were polishing up résumés, updating their skills, and asking anyone they knew for job leads. "There was a real sense that if you didn't get another job quickly, everything good would be taken by the time they came to you," Sandi said.

Then she took a deeper look.

For the past twelve years, the reliable, good job in Detroit had been taking a steady, psychic toll. Sandi enjoyed the work but felt that she was sacrificing herself, devoting her best energy to the studio in corporate America instead of the adventure that tugged at her heart. "When I was laid off," she told me, "I realized that this might be my last chance to create something really different."

What Sandi really wanted was to experience small-town life on the road, in a way that would allow her to create lasting memories. She wanted to find herself, and the specific quest took shape as she thought about a dream she'd had for a long time but never pursued. Sandi would travel in a slow, thoughtful journey on the classic American highway known as Route 66, documenting the trip along the way.

The more she reflected on her dream, the more it took root. In a journey of reinvention, she set off to see America in slow motion. Over the next six weeks, she took sixty thousand photographs, one every few seconds from a camera she mounted on the dashboard of her camper. She slept in campsites, rising early to get back on the highway. After years of following the same routine of toiling away in a corporate office, the new way of life was thrilling. She'd been missing something, she realized, and the road seemed to open with possibilities as she made her way through the changing landscapes.

☻

Around the same time as Sandi's layoff and Big Idea, a young university graduate in England was in a funk. Tom Allen had everything going for him, or so it seemed. Yet as we see with other people who undertake a quest, he struggled with a sense of dissatisfaction and a deep yearning to break out of what had become a traditional life path. "I was sick of not being in control of my own decisions," he said. "I had that horrible feeling that other people were steering my life."

The inspiration for Tom's journey came from a job-screening process he went through around the time of his graduation. He'd sailed through the company's exams and impressed the human resources rep who interviewed him. "We like to invest in our employees," the rep told him, which sounded good to Tom. "We want people to commit for the long term," the rep continued, which didn't sound as good.

When his interviewer called back to officially offer an employment contract, Tom was surprised to find himself asking for time to think it over. He'd won out over several other candidates in precisely the field he'd trained for. True, the work wasn't highly engaging, but with a good salary and job security, what was the problem?

The problem was that Tom had another idea in mind, and the idea wouldn't leave him. When he finally turned down the job, explaining that he wanted to see more of the world first, he could picture the HR rep shaking his head on the other end of the call. "Better get it out of your system," the interviewer said. "It's a shame to pass up a good job."

Better get it out of your system. Tom wasn't sure if his longing to explore was something he had to get out of his system, but he knew it wasn't going away. A cycling trip around the world was just the kind of ludicrous idea that made sense to a young guy who wanted to do something different. He managed to rope in a couple of friends, Mark and Andy, and the three set out on a journey they expected to take at least one year.

If the idea was ludicrous, the planning was almost nonexistent. Tom was the de facto leader of the trip, yet had little cycling experience. A previous jaunt to the Scottish Highlands had resulted in confidence but not much knowledge of traveling in difficult conditions where he didn't speak the language. He knew nothing about gear. His travels abroad were limited to a few countries that weren't very challenging. In his own words, he was "an absolute beginner and 100 percent naive." Nevertheless, the group left their English village, traveling south through the countryside, on to the Netherlands, and eventually to Turkey and more challenging destinations.

The joys of inexperienced cyclists traversing unfamiliar regions with little money quickly gave way to weariness. Missing his girlfriend, Mark returned to England, leaving Tom and Andy behind. Holed up for the snowy winter in Tbilisi, Georgia, Andy decided to stay on while Tom continued the journey alone.

A documentary film he made after the trip shows Tom cycling through the desert of Sudan, camera mounted to his bike's handlebars. He has no map and travels village to village, looking haggard. Feeling ill, he at one point opts for a local treatment that involves bloodletting. Alas, the treatment is unsuccessful, and in another village he learns he has malaria. It's rough going, but through it all we can see Tom gaining confidence and experience.

As rough as it was, after a year of intentional homelessness, Tom had adapted to the challenges of life on the road. The low points of struggling up hills and cycling into deserts were offset by moments of joy at realizing how far from England he'd come. Strangers would flag him down and offer bottles of beer. He would gaze out at winding roads leading to snow-capped mountains, seeing new parts of the world with the eyes of an experienced traveler. Gone was the naive young man who had left his home on a whim. Tom Allen was now road-tested and flying high on his bike as he moved from country to country. "It's so much more important to do what your heart's telling you," he said to the handheld camera. The quest was under way.

"The Sense of Being at the Reins of My Life"

When Sandi talked about the moment she decided to put the job search on hold and pursue a big adventure, she described it as "the sense of being at the reins of my life." She was taking control as part of a broader life mission to reinvent herself. Twelve years had gone by at GM, and Sandi realized if the change hadn't come along, another dozen years might pass in the same circumstances. "I had zero clue how to do it," she told me when we met up in Toronto, "but I was driven by the desire to avoid looking back years later and calling myself a chickenshit for not using this opportunity for something."

She began the journey as a project of self-discovery and documentation, but the biggest surprise was a new career. Upon returning to her native Canada, she began receiving offers to speak and submit her photography to major exhibits. One of her photos landed on the cover of a prominent art magazine. At the same time, she pursued a new opportunity as a tour guide, leading groups throughout the Maritime Provinces where she'd grown up. The opportunity allowed her to work part-time during the best season of the year for touring, and still provided plenty of time to pursue her art and travels. Sandi's reinvention had come full circle, in a totally different way than expected.

Looking back now, she feels only satisfaction in making the U-turn to pursue a quest instead of immediately looking for another job. "We get one ride in life," she says. "I'm so glad I did this."

Looking Within

Whether you're trying to decide on your next steps, filtering out dissenting voices, or just nudging yourself along a set course, it helps to consult your internal compass. Consider these questions for self-reflection 101.

How am I feeling?
Your final decision may not be based entirely on feelings, but feelings can be a good overall temperature check. What makes you happy, and what makes you sad? Are you eager to make progress, or are you deferring the next part of the task?

What do I want, really?
In my case, I often want to get things done and move ahead on projects. In those cases, the answer to my "What do I want?" question involves making a list of what I hope to accomplish. I base this list on the two or three most important projects on my mind that day, and I know that if I can complete them or at least make good progress during the day, I'll feel better later. Sometimes I want something completely different, and by thinking about these questions, I may realize that I don't feel very productive. I may need to rest, or exercise, or just go to the coffee shop to read for the afternoon.

What is my identity?
Who are you? What do you want to do, ultimately? Your identity shapes everything about you—how you spend your time, your work, your priorities, and everything else. If you already have a good idea of who you are, take the time to remind yourself of that image as you plan next steps. If you can focus on what's important to you in the midst of bad news, and that image brings you comfort, you know you're doing something right.

Can I change the terms of this situation?
There are two kinds of challenges: those where you can take action to remedy the situation, and those where you're relatively powerless. It's always good to know which kind of challenge you're facing. If you can influence the situation for the better, you can then make a plan for change. If you can't, then you can move to a plan for acceptance of the bad news.

You won't always have the answers to everything. But when you follow the path indicated by your inner compass, you can deal with the external challenges as they come.

Start with Why

As I talked with Sandi, Tom, and many others who'd stepped away from a conventional life to pursue something different, I wanted to understand *why*. In some cases, the choices that people made were serious and consequential. They had to give something up to achieve the life experiences they wanted. What causes someone to undertake a big adventure for little reward—in many cases with a real chance of failure or at least major sacrifice?

The answers seemed elusive. When I asked the *why* question of people all over the world, I noticed that the answers were often circular, perhaps even unsatisfactory. "It made sense at the time," some people said, in an answer that could just as easily have been "I wanted to do it, so I did."

I found the real answer as I dug deeper into the mix of frustration and inspiration that drives action. Most of the people I talked to, in one way or another, had been dissatisfied with their normal lives. They wanted something deeper than

they had known or experienced, and they either found it or
created it.

"Something had to give."

Sasha Martin, a thirty-year-old mother in Tulsa, Oklahoma,
described the beginnings of an ambitious culinary project as a
means of fighting back against complacency. "Something had
to give," she said. "I was settling into the comfortable rut of
wife and mother, but losing my sense of adventure."

Losing something—in this case, the sense of adventure—
and going back in an effort to reclaim it is a common charac-
teristic of beginning a quest. In quests of old, the hero had
to travel across distant lands in search of reclaiming a grail
or key. These days, we often have to recover something more
intangible but no less important. Many of us undertake an adventure to rediscover our sense of self.

"A crazy idea that wouldn't leave me alone."

Nate Damm was a twenty-year-old from Portland, Maine,
who couldn't get something out of his head. "At first," he told
me, "it was just a crazy idea that wouldn't leave me alone until
I did it. It nagged me daily for about two years before I actually decided to go for it." One day he set out to turn the idea
into action, one step at a time from Maine to California. Over
the next seven months, he walked across the United States.

"I just couldn't live that way anymore."

Travis Eneix, who weighed four hundred pounds and committed to practicing tai chi and writing down everything he
ate for one thousand days, describes how he finally came to

the point where he had to change. "I just couldn't live that way anymore," he said. "I didn't want to make a small adjustment; I had to completely shift directions to find a new way of life."

Lesson: When you sense discontent, pay attention. The answer isn't always "go for it" (though often it is), but you shouldn't neglect the stirring. Properly examined, feelings of unease can lead to a new life of purpose.

Notice: Action Needed ("What if . . . ?")

Discontent is a powerful spark. When you're filled with a sense of dissatisfaction that isn't easily resolved, you may start wondering about making some changes. On its own, however, discontent is not sufficient to start a fire—or inspire a quest. Lots of people are walking around unhappy, but most don't make radical changes in their lives, especially to the point of pursuing a quest. Discontent may be the instigator, but what is the motivator? What causes someone to take action?

If you want to get the embers burning, you have to blend dissatisfaction with inspiration, and then you have to connect the dissatisfaction to a greater purpose.

Mash-up:
Dissatisfaction + Big Idea + Willingness to Take Action = New Adventure

After being laid off, Sandi was less than excited at the prospect of competing for another job right away. But that wasn't all—she also had an idea in mind. The dream to travel Route 66 was calling her name, and she answered the call by purchasing a camper and announcing her plans to everyone she knew.

Others began the pursuit of a dream by asking "What if . . . ?" and found a way to make the preposterous come true.

What if I could walk across an entire country?

Would it really be possible to produce a symphony that requires one thousand performers?

Could I stop illegal logging by climbing to the top of a eucalyptus tree . . . and staying there for a whole year?

Why did Tom Allen, who left England for life on the road, turn down his prospects for a good job and an easy life? He uses the word *discomfort*. "I felt a deep discomfort with the life I'd been prescribed. I had some preexisting interests and desires, so seeing that others had made that same leap, I packed it all in and followed a dream of my own."

Dissatisfaction: check.

Reexamining personal interests: check.

Inspired by role models: check.

Finally, the most critical step: Tom took action.

TOM'S ACTION PLAN

Precipitating Event: Graduation and a job offer he didn't want.

Underlying Value: Longing for something more. ("It's about letting a little risk into your life.")

Big Idea: See the world by bicycle!

Action: Leave England, head for the Netherlands and beyond.

SANDI'S ACTION PLAN

Precipitating Event: Job loss.

Underlying Value: Fear of regret and excitement over the road trip. ("The sense of being at the reins of my life.")
Big Idea: Photograph America's Route 66!
Action: Buy a camper, plan the journey, hit the road.

"Why Can't We All Be Happy?"

Juno Kim was twenty-seven years old when she left her stable engineering job in South Korea to travel the world. Coming from a culture that values conformity and adherence to the norm, Juno had a hard time explaining her motivations to her family—especially her father. When she first revealed that she was unhappy with the engineering job and wanted to do something else, she was told flat-out: "You're not special. Only special people can pursue happiness, and you're not one of them."

Undaunted, she left anyway, traveling to other countries in Asia and eventually even farther, visiting twenty-four countries in three years. "To many Koreans," she explained when I visited Seoul, "pursuing happiness is not a priority. It's a 'hippie' thing. They work to live, and live to work. I wanted to reclaim my creativity, inspiration, and happiness. Why can't I be one of the few? And why can't we all be happy?"

Years later, Juno is still on the road, working independently as a writer and photographer. Though her father remains uncomfortable with her travels, over time her mother and brother have grown to support her. Just as important, Juno now receives emails and letters from other people who would like to follow in her path, especially Asian women who are inspired by the idea that not all backpackers are from Western countries. She tells them that happiness is a choice, and that no one has be special to pursue a dream.

If you've ever felt a strange sense of sadness or alienation, there's a potential way out of the confusion—just shift this feeling to a sense of purpose. It's not all about *happiness*, although happiness often results from doing something you love. Instead, it's about challenge and fulfillment, finding the perfect combination of striving and achievement that comes from reaching a big goal.

Metaphorically, discontent is the match and inspiration is the kindling. When discontent leads to excitement, that's when you know you've found your pursuit. As we'll see in the next chapter, it may even feel like a calling.

Recall Sandi Wheaton's words. When she set out to chart her own course, she described it as "the sense of being at the reins of my life." Other people had been in control of her destiny before, but no longer. It was now all up to her.

Remember

Many quests begin from a sense of discontent or alienation. If you find yourself feeling discontented, pay attention to the reasons why.

Add action to discontent: Find a way to *do something* about the uncertainty you feel.

Asking yourself a series of questions ("What do I want?" "How am I feeling?" and so forth) can help you find your next steps.

Chapter 3

The Calling

Here is a test to find out whether your mission in life is complete. If you're alive, it isn't.

—LAUREN BACALL

Lesson: EVERYONE HAS A CALLING.
FOLLOW *YOUR* PASSION.

There's a story in the Torah about twelve spies who are sent out from the desert to investigate the land of Canaan. They complete their mission and are entranced by what they find. The land, as the saying goes, is flowing in milk and honey, with good phone reception even in the tunnels. It's a wonderful, magical place even better than Disney World.

The spies report this information back to the camp. "Wonderful news!" the elders say.

But the report goes on to say that, in addition to the milk and honey, there are giants and fortified cities. Life in the desert isn't much fun, but getting to Canaan could be dangerous. Ten of the twelve spies end their consulting report with an ominous recommendation: Moving into the promised land is just too difficult. Better to play it safe and not fight for the land of our dreams.

Two of the twelve spies file a dissenting report. "Yes, it's tough," they say. Those cities, those giants—there will indeed be challenges. "But we can do it!" they tell the others. "Let's proceed."

Alas, the possibility of danger outweighs the promise of hope. The people choose to believe the pessimists, and they miss the Disney World experience for forty more years. The ten spies who warned of failure die of plague. Of the twelve, only the two dissenters later make it across.

❂

Hannah Pasternak referred to this story when talking with me about her upcoming move to Israel. As a young American of Israeli heritage, she'd long held an affection for her faraway homeland. As she was reading the Torah one day and came across the story, she realized that she was just like the spies who'd seen the promised land but then searched for reasons to stay away.

Hannah decided to bring some risk into her life. Not only would she move to Israel, where she'd never lived, but she'd begin her new life by hiking the country's National Trail, a thousand-kilometer journey that would take up to two months.

Just as general dissatisfaction is often not enough to spur action, being emotionally impacted by a significant event may not be sufficient, either. You have to choose to *respond* to the event. Hannah spent the months leading up to departure learning more about family history. She took Hebrew lessons and prepared for the physically challenging hike.

The preparation was helpful, she said later, but the decision to go was far more important. She wasn't like the ten spies who were frightened by a new opportunity. Like the two spies who went against the majority opinion, and whose ancestors exhibited a high level of risk tolerance, Hannah would face her fears and embrace the challenge. Instead of uncertainty, she felt a sense of peace.

When she thought about moving to Israel and hiking the trail, she couldn't get the idea out of her head. Life in America was fine and well, but when she considered living in a foreign land and experiencing a different way of life, she felt a pull that she couldn't ignore.

Others I talked to experienced a similar draw. They had a life that was relatively satisfying, but waiting beyond their comfort zones was something better. Scott Harrison, a friend who started the organization Charity: Water, originally arrived in West Africa on a search for penance. After years of debauchery as a New York City nightclub promoter, he found his calling while bouncing around a Land Rover on the muddy roads of Monrovia, Liberia. There's a whole world without clean water, Scott realized, and he wanted to find a way to bring it to them.

I watched Scott struggle with forming his initial message. One day he spoke with us about a dream he had. In the dream he saw a stadium filled with people. It was hard to explain, but Scott believed that his life was somehow connected to those people, and he had to do anything he could to help them. Scott would spend the next decade building a $100 million organization, aiming for 100 percent coverage of clean water in Ethiopia and elsewhere. The work was enormously successful, helping millions of people—far more than enough to fill the stadium he'd envisioned—but it all began with his responding to that pull.

Not every calling is religious or explicitly moral. People who are nonreligious, or whose religious practice is more personal, also speak of embracing a calling when they inch closer toward the goals they've set. Whether it's writing, crafting, or saving the world, submitting to a purpose greater than yourself can prove fulfilling. It's a combination of destiny and determined free will. No matter which you believe—and perhaps in the end it's a bit of both—those who pursue a calling feel a deep sense of mission.

For some, that feeling can lead to lifelong sacrifice and discovery.

A Taste of Freedom

John Francis was an environmentalist before he knew what the word meant. An African American man who grew up in Philadelphia before migrating west to California, John had been sensitive to the world of nature for as long as he could remember. In 1971, two oil tankers collided in the San Francisco Bay, spilling a half million gallons of crude oil into the waters near the Golden Gate Bridge. John was angry and saddened by the oil spill, but he also felt frustrated. What can one person do?

The idea came to him in much the same way I thought about visiting every country—it was a notion that seemed crazy at first but wouldn't go away. Still disturbed by the oil spill a year later, John was hanging out with his friend Jean one night when he blurted out his idea. "We could stop driving cars. Stop riding in them too," he said.

Jean agreed, but then reality kicked in. "That would be a good thing to do when we have more money."

"Yeah," said John. "It's probably not realistic." But the idea stayed with him, and like many other crazy ideas, there was something to it.

A few weeks later, John was headed to a party at a night-club in a neighboring town twenty miles away, and he decided to walk instead of drive. Leaving the car keys behind and putting a daypack on his back, he hit the road and started off toward the party.

As you might expect, it takes a long time to walk twenty miles. Turning down offers for rides, John finally stopped at a fast food restaurant around midnight, where the teenager at the counter refused to take his money after learning how far he'd walked. By the time he made it to the nightclub, it was one a.m. and the band was winding down with their final encore. No matter. He'd made it.

The next day, John checked into a motel, took a hot shower, and spent the afternoon recharging by the pool—before heading out to walk the twenty miles back home. It was physically harder than the first walk, since his muscles weren't used to such effort, but mentally he began adjusting to the idea of slow-distance travel.

It's not every day that someone decides to walk forty miles round-trip to a nightclub, so his friends had arranged a welcoming celebration in light of the achievement. Champagne was served, and the group asked John to explain more about his crazy expedition.

That's when John said something that surprised even him: "It was a taste of freedom. For a while I hoped I didn't have to come back."

The taste of freedom was enticing. "I have taken the first

step on a journey that will shape my life," he wrote in a journal that later became a memoir. "I cannot stop now."

❂

After the experience of walking forty miles to the dance party, John had difficulty readjusting to normal life. One day he decided to keep walking indefinitely. Wherever he needed to go and whatever he needed to do, he'd find a way to get there on foot.

Learning to walk everywhere was surprisingly easy, but adjusting to life without cars took some time. John's job as a concert promoter didn't last. His friendships changed since he was no longer able to make last-minute plans. When his friends went to a movie at a theater that was twenty-five miles away, John had to plan a day in advance to walk to meet them.

Some people found his decision to avoid cars inspiring, but others were confused and even hurt. Drivers would stop to offer him rides, John would decline and explain about his protest of the oil spill, and the drivers would be offended. "Do you think you're better than me?" some asked.

John shared his impressions of the early experience in his journal. "I have taken a stand that challenges a way of life," he wrote. "It is no wonder that people challenge me. I am challenging myself."

Yet the greatest frustration wasn't the people who didn't get it; it was that he didn't know how to explain what he was doing. "I am unable to articulate beyond a simple phrase about why I walk . . . . I start to feel that each step taken is part of an invisible journey for which there is no map and few road signs. I am not sure I am prepared."

As John was processing his new way of life, his mother said something offhand that reframed the whole idea. On a phone call placed to her home in Philadelphia, he told her about how happy he was to walk everywhere. But something in his voice sounded off, and his perceptive mother picked up on it. "You know, Johnny," she said. "When a person is really happy they don't have to tell people about it. It just shows."

Unbeknown to her at the time, this conversation inspired a whole new phase in John's pursuit of purpose.

On John's twenty-seventh birthday, he decided to remain silent for the day—a gift, as he put it, to everyone who'd been listening to him chatter and argue about his new phase of life. He walked out to the beach, five hours away. He spent the day journaling and painting, falling asleep on the sand and staying until the next day, and then the next. Three days later he finally headed home, but something had changed. Several more weeks went by, all without John saying a word. Now he knew what his real challenge was: Not only would he forgo riding in cars, but he'd also live his life in total silence.

Not everyone understood John's new silence, and just like when he started walking everywhere, some people were angry. But since he wasn't able to respond, at least not in the usual manner, he found this form of protest different from when he was just not riding in cars. As we'll see a bit later on, the new practice of avoiding mechanical transport *and* remaining silent became a seventeen-year quest of its own—but for now, John was just trying to adopt an unconventional lifestyle rooted in his beliefs about the environment. "Not speaking precludes argument," he wrote in his journal. "And the silence instructs me to listen."

Go Big (aka "Unconventional Heart Surgery")

When I wrote my first book on unconventional ideas, I made the mistake of qualifying a passage by saying "Still, you probably wouldn't want an unconventional heart surgeon." Since then I've heard from five heart surgeons who wrote in separately to say, "Wait, that's me!"

One of them was Dr. Mani Sivasubramanian, who lives in India. His business card reads "Pediatric Surgeon and Social Entrepreneur." Dr. Mani created a foundation to provide health care access for low-income children. The other unconventional heart surgeons told me that advances in their profession have all come about by thinking differently about how they care for patients.

Lesson learned: Never say never. If running a marathon, starting a charity, or anything else in this book seems tame to you, take it up a level:

Find a cure for a disease. Steven Kirsch, who was diagnosed with a rare blood disease, is attempting to find a cure for himself and everyone else with the same condition.

Become a ninja. Twenty-nine-year-old Izzy Arkin quit his job and moved to Kyoto, Japan, to study martial arts full-time. His goal isn't just to master karate—he wants to become an actual ninja, just like he dreamed when he was eight years old. (It's a work in progress.)

Enter a monastery. Former Wall Street banker Rasanath Dasa left his career after becoming disillusioned with the industry and sensing the loss of his soul. He entered a monastery in the East Village and became an urban monk.

In other words, please don't limit yourself to something you find in these pages. If you've got a bigger and better idea, proceed! Teach the rest of us a lesson.

Follow *Your* Passion

In an interview for *Rolling Stone,* Bob Dylan was asked about the word *calling*. "Everybody has a calling," he said. "Some have a high calling, some have a low calling. Everybody is called but few are chosen. There's a lot of distraction for people, so you might not ever find the real you. A lot of people don't."

When asked how he would describe his own calling, here's how he answered.

> *Mine? Not any different than anybody else's. Some people are called to be a good sailor. Some people have a calling to be a good tiller of the land. Some people are called to be a good friend. You have to be the best at whatever you are called at. Whatever you do. You ought to be the best at it—highly skilled. It's about confidence, not arrogance. You have to know that you're the best whether anybody else tells you that or not.*

Embracing a calling is about being the best at something, or doing something that you feel no one else can do. Not necessarily in a competitive manner, where you have to beat someone else, but according to your own standard of what you know is true.

Some of us discover a quest, and sometimes the quest discovers us. Whichever is the case with you, once you identify your calling, don't lose sight of it.

◓

Jiro Ono lives in Tokyo and operates the three-star Michelin restaurant Sukiyabashi Jiro. At more than seventy years old, he has spent his adult life preparing and serving sushi with unwavering passion. He is absolutely, positively committed to the task at hand. Meals at his restaurant take only fifteen minutes to eat at a simple counter. There is a set menu of sushi (No appetizers! Nothing ordered à la carte!) and reservations are taken up to a year in advance. The bill is approximately $300 per person, no credit cards accepted.

During much of a documentary film that portrays his family and restaurant, Jiro repeatedly declares his dedication to his work, how he values his skill above all else, and so on. It's noble but a bit monotonous. Then we see him come alive as he talks about what really drives him: the fish itself. "When we have a good tuna, I feel great," he says with a smile. "I feel victorious!"

I laughed out loud when I heard Jiro talking about feeling victorious over a good tuna. But I also got the message: The man loves what he does.

There's a popular online video of a train enthusiast who spots a particularly exciting carriage coming his way down the tracks. "OH MY GOD!" he shouts. "I've been waiting for this moment for months, and it's finally here. I am finally gonna get a Heritage Unit on camera! Whoo-hoo! Yeah!"

Don't relate to the excitement? Don't know what a Heritage Unit is? That's because you're not a train enthusiast like Mark McDonough, the guy who made the original "Excited Train Guy" video.*

The point is, maybe your heart doesn't race over vintage train carriages, and maybe you don't feel passionate about tuna—but that's how you'll feel when you find *your* quest. It will be big,

---

*The most popular "Excited Train" video is actually an homage to the lesser-known original. To see both of them, Google "excited train guy."

exciting, and maybe even a little scary or overwhelming. Deep down, you'll be drawn to it in a way that feels authentic and long lasting.

Back to You

Your calling might not require you to walk the earth in silence for seventeen years, and it might not beckon you to Tokyo in search of the world's most uncompromising tuna. You might not pack your bags for Israel or anywhere else that seems far away.

Nevertheless, there's a mission out there that is greater than yourself. Whether or not you think of it in spiritual terms, a true calling will challenge and thrill you.

A true calling also involves trade-offs. If your dream is to take an extra hour for your lunch break and walk in the park, it's more of a task than a mission. A real dream requires investment, and often it calls for sacrifice—yet when you feel excited about something, even if it doesn't make sense to others, the journey will produce its own rewards.

Many years ago, when she was flying high and challenging assumptions of what women could do in a male-dominated world, Amelia Earhart might have put it best: "When a great adventure is offered, you don't refuse it."

Remember

———

Hannah was challenged by reading about the spies of Canaan. When her inspiration finally took hold, she found her next step.

"The taste of freedom" that John Francis found was enticing—and seemingly addictive. Once he had it, he couldn't return to his old way of life.

If you're not excited about tuna or trains, what *are* you excited about? Be attentive to what happens when you lose yourself in the moment.

Dispatch

Courage

The first time I went to Dubai, I landed late at night. I arrived at the airport after a long journey that had taken me from the United States to Denmark, then to Athens, and finally down to the Persian Gulf. It was my first time in the region, and only the second big trip I'd taken since deciding to visit every country.

Most airports are restricted to flights that land or take off in the daytime and early evening hours. Once midnight hits, it's lights-out at the terminal in much of the world. But in Dubai, the opposite is true: Crashing the town at one a.m. seemed perfectly normal, as crowds of Bangladeshi and Filipino passengers descended from planes at remote gates and were bussed to immigration.

I stepped outside the terminal into a hall of rental car companies. I'd arranged to rent a car for the following five days, but the company whose name was listed on my reservation email was nowhere to be seen. After a fruitless search, I found a guy who knew a guy who knew another guy who would rent me a car with a different company. It sounded random but I followed him to another counter in the outdoor lot, avoiding the throng of arriving passengers queuing for taxis and immigrant workers waiting for the bus.

Despite the runaround, the paperwork to get the car was surprisingly easy. My handler said good-bye and I took a deep breath. *Ready for this? I asked myself.* I was heading to Deira, a market district that was reported to contain a number of budget hotels. I studied the map I'd received at the airport and turned the key. It was now nearly three a.m. and raining, yet the street was teeming with vehicles. Fortunately, I found my location—or at least, I found a parking spot on a street with hotels—and then after a couple of false starts, I found a room for $40 a night. *Success!*

Late the next morning I checked out and prepared for a long drive. I'd be heading out of Dubai and into the desert. Equipped with the map and a bag of samosas, I drove out of the city and onto the national highway. For the next three days I drove through the country, visiting all seven emirates before returning to Dubai. I spent the night at a seaman's hotel in Fujairah, and I drove through part of Oman, a neighboring country that also maintains a small enclave within the United Arab Emirates.

The rental car was equipped with an annoying *ding!* sound that erupted whenever I drove above the speed limit. Once I was out of the city, however, the six-lane highway was flat and wide open. Cars would zoom past me even as I pushed the limit. Finally I gave up and joined them, deciding to ignore the *ding!* as I continued down the road. I felt a sense of freedom being out in the desert. *This is actually happening,* I thought. *I can do this.*

On the third day of the journey, I found myself lost as the sun was going down. *Would I run out of fuel? I wondered. Did I know how to find my way back?*

Yet instead of worrying, I felt surprisingly peaceful. I was on the road, just as I'd planned. I had figured out how to navigate a new environment, and the accomplishment gave me courage for the next steps. All would be well.

❧

Years later I met someone who was getting ready to head out on her first big trip. "Compared to where you go," she said, "it's no big deal."

Then I heard from someone who wrote in to say he'd "only" been to twenty countries. What? Twenty countries is great. Plenty of people never go anywhere.

Embracing new things often requires us to embrace our fears, however trivial they may seem. You deal with fear not by pretending it doesn't exist, but by refusing to give it decision-making authority. When you venture to new lands for the first time, it is a big deal.

Chapter 4

Defining Moments

He had decided to live forever, or die in the attempt.
—JOSEPH HELLER

Lesson: EVERY DAY MATTERS. THE EMOTIONAL
AWARENESS OF MORTALITY CAN HELP US
PURSUE A GOAL.

The rule of improv theater is to always keep the story going. You finish your part and ask, "And then?" The idea is that every story can be extended, sometimes with unexpected results.

But if you want to understand a life story, you don't look forward—you look back. Instead of asking "And then?" you ask, "But why?"

In *The $100 Startup,* I shared a few stories of people who started successful businesses after being fired or laid off from their jobs. These stories were inspiring, but in some ways I was even more inspired by those who'd created their own freedom without such an obvious push. When everything is going along swimmingly, yet someone still feels the need to change it up, that's when you know they're serious.

❂

Any given moment can change your life. For some people it's a conversation that opens the doors of possibility: a new business opportunity, perhaps, or a new relationship. For others it's the sudden shift in perspective: *I don't have to live like this anymore.* For Tom Allen in England, the tipping point was hearing the news of a good job offer, yet feeling strangely discomforted by the idea that his life was now set in place for the foreseeable future.

In the case of Adam Warner, his defining moment was far more serious.

Adam met Meghan Baker when they were both working as English teachers in South Korea. They fell in love and began planning a future together. Adam was American and had been enjoying life outside the routine he knew at home. Meghan was Canadian and planned to return to school to become a nurse.

Meghan had a life list of goals she'd been working on. Much of the list was fairly typical. Among other things, she hoped to run a half marathon, learn another language, visit thirty countries, take the train across Canada, and "own a little cottage by the lake." Other goals were more altruistic, including volunteering overseas and supporting local organizations.

Sadly, one year after meeting Adam, Meghan was diagnosed with breast cancer at the age of twenty-six. The couple relocated back to North America, Adam to his hometown of Washington, D.C., and Meghan to Ontario to receive treatment. Whenever possible, Adam traveled to Canada to be close to her, and he eventually moved to Detroit so he could more easily visit across the border.

Meghan's cancer was fast spreading, and despite numerous

rounds of treatment, a year later she received a terminal diagnosis and was shifted to hospice care. One of the goals she'd written on her list was "Get married," to which she added in parentheses "No pressure, Adam."

He didn't need to be convinced. Adam and Meghan were married at a home ceremony in Ontario on March 28, 2010. One month later, Meghan died.

There is no shortcut around grief, even when a death is somewhat expected. At an especially young age, Adam had lost the love of his life. Yet even through his sadness, he now had a focus of his own. He would take over the list of goals from Meghan and make it his pursuit, completing as many aspirational tasks as he could and choosing his next steps based on his young wife's dreams.

This wasn't a revelation that grew on him over time; he knew it right away. "The idea gave me solace right after her death," he told me. "Walking away from the hospital, I knew that I had to adopt her goals as my own. This would be my project and my focus for as long as it took."

Two weeks after Meghan's death, Adam created a Facebook page where he published Meghan's goals along with his own progress. Six months later, he was volunteering at a school in India. He felt as though Meghan was with him, sharing his surprise at the ordered chaos of life in Delhi, and joining him as he rode eighteen-hour trains throughout the country. He grieved for Meghan every day, yet he also felt purposeful in following her original list.

Adam's story was brought to my attention by one of my blog readers, who wrote to say that Meghan's life, not her death, inspired the quest. Adam's friends agree that his pursuit of Meghan's goals has given him a sense of purpose, changing his life for the better. The blog originally started by Meghan is now updated by Adam. He went to a Blue Jays game in Toronto, something Meghan wasn't able to do before her illness rapidly progressed. He got more serious about running and completed the half marathon. He is—slowly—learning to sew and knit.

As I read through the blog, one story stood out. On a day before Meghan had shifted to hospice care, she'd just completed radiation treatment and wanted to go outside. For her, a short walk in the city didn't count as being outdoors, so she took Adam to a nearby lake and they went out on a canoe. They went farther out than they'd planned, and when the time came to return Meghan was tired and needed Adam to do most of the rowing. It was just like Meghan, he wrote later. When they'd both started running a couple of years earlier, before she was sick, Adam would run two miles and Meghan would run three. She always went all-in on everything she did. She didn't save anything for later. This was how she lived her life, and Adam hoped to share this message with the rest of the world.

When I caught up with Adam and reminded him of this story, he smiled.

"When does it feel worth it?" I asked him.

"Every time I mark off one of her goals," he said. "I think Meghan unintentionally chose goals that would make anyone a better version of themselves. I feel like I grow with each notch."

The Emotional Awareness of Mortality

This is a fact: All of us will someday die. Yet not all of us live in a state of active awareness of this reality. In the words of a great Bob Dylan song, "He not busy being born is busy dying," and perhaps some of us are busier than others.

Kathleen Taylor has spent nearly twenty years working in hospice. She started as a bedside counselor, doing what she could to comfort people in the final chapter of their lives. If it sounds depressing, it's not—Kathleen finds the work fulfilling and meaningful. When people ask what she likes about it, she has a great answer: "At the end of their lives, people are incapable of bullshit. The normal distractions fall off the map. You can't help but be yourself."

Many of the people I talked to for this book seemed to have an early awareness of the end of life. They didn't wait until death was around the corner to reflect on what matters. Instead, they chose to take life by the reins as soon as they could. As much as it sounds trite to "live like you're dying" or "live every day as if it were your last," that's exactly what many people obsessed with a quest do. This shift from an *intellectual* awareness that we will someday die to an *emotional* awareness can be a guiding light to discovering what really matters.

> *Intellectual Awareness of Mortality:* "I know that no one lives forever."
> *Emotional Awareness of Mortality:* "I know that I will someday die."

Once you start thinking about your own mortality, the small things just don't matter anymore. This new awareness may come in response to an external event, such as the death or sudden illness of a friend, or from confronting a serious health problem. Other times, there's a stirring of the soul that increases in tempo until it's impossible to ignore. Whatever it is, the more we're emotionally aware of our own mortality, the more we feel compelled to live with a sense of purpose.

John Francis, who would later walk the earth under a vow of silence for nearly twenty years, was sensitive to death for as long as he could remember. As a six-year-old child he'd seen a robin crushed by a car, and the bird's death haunted him for weeks. The next year his aunt died from tuberculosis, and he remembers his parents carrying him home from the funeral. He was so overcome from grief that he couldn't walk.

As John was beginning his quest years later, he was told by his doctor that he had swollen lymph nodes on his neck. He had surgery and was relieved to learn that the nodes were benign, but the experience shook him. Quoting from a Japanese film about a bureaucrat who discovers a reason to live just as he's faced with imminent death, John wrote in his journal: "How interesting it is that men seldom find the true value of life until they are faced with death."

Juno Kim, who left a corporate job in South Korea to travel independently, saw both her parents successfully treated for cancer in the same year. "Watching them survive, I began thinking: We are not young and healthy forever." Along with her own dissatisfaction with the usual career path in Korea, this observation led Juno to embark on an odyssey that led her to more than twenty countries.

"All These Things I Haven't Yet Done"

Phoebe Snetsinger led a fairly normal life until the age of thirty-four. The daughter of Midwestern advertising icon Leo Burnett, she grew up in a 1940s-era traditional home, first in the suburbs of Chicago and then on a farm in northern Illinois. Phoebe headed east to Swarthmore College in Pennsylvania, taught science and math at a girls' school after graduation, and then—as was the custom of the time—married and had children, leaving her job to focus on raising her family while her husband Dave worked.

By her early thirties, Phoebe and Dave had relocated to Minnesota with their four children. In her memoir, *Birding on Borrowed Time,* Phoebe describes the moment she first became captivated by birds as an "awakening." A neighbor was an avid birder, and one day while they were outside he handed Phoebe his binoculars, pointed to "a fiery-orange male Blackburnian Warbler," and described its features. Phoebe hadn't give much thought to birds until then, and she'd never heard of warblers, but from that day on she was hooked. She began making field trips with her friend to the surrounding areas, where she learned to look at birds in a whole new way.

Phoebe describes these early days as a "magical season of wonder," a thrilling euphoria hitting her as she discovered a focal point that had been missing for much of her life. The family moved to St. Louis, Missouri, for Dave's job, and Phoebe joined a group of birders who introduced her to the local area.

The initial awakening eventually shifted to a full-fledged pursuit. In one year, Phoebe set the Missouri state record by seeing 275 distinct bird species. She began hopping across the border to Illinois, working on the record there as well. As her children grew and needed less attention, she began branching out, making trips throughout the country.

Mexico was next, followed by the Galápagos Islands and a brief visit to mainland Ecuador. These were family trips that included birding, but after an extended visit to Kenya, Phoebe's fixation entered a new phase. Dave came along for the first two weeks ("Days of simply astounding birding!" she wrote in her journal), but Phoebe stayed on for an additional two weeks. Every day she'd leave with a tour leader and be gone until late afternoon, racking up lists of new species and gaining more confidence in her identification skills.

At the end of the trip she returned home reluctantly, with the strong desire to get back to the field as quickly as possible. Even at home, birding became a full-time passion. In the days before computers were in common use, Phoebe created an extensive documentation system compiled by hand on index cards. Hour upon hour was spent cataloguing the six hundred birds she'd seen in Kenya, as well as the six hundred she'd racked up in North America.

As Phoebe spent more and more time in her study, her family complained that she was spending so much time documenting the bird sightings that had occurred on her journey that she may as well have been back in Africa. This relentless focus created its own set of problems later—but for now, there was no turning back. Phoebe would devote the rest of her life to seeing more birds than anyone else.

After the first big foreign trip to Africa for a month of nonstop birding, she was addicted. New trips were quickly planned, both in the United States and abroad. Dave was settling into a new role at work, and the four children were nearly all grown. As Phoebe put it in her memoir, "Birds and travel were becoming the focus of life." But then a diagnosis of melanoma threatened her plans, since the cancer was nearly always terminal. Visits to three separate oncologists produced the same verdict. She'd most certainly be dead within a year.*

Happily, the death sentence was premature. After deciding to forgo experimental treatment in favor of living actively for as long as she could, Phoebe was unexpectedly given a clean bill of health. Three oncologists had predicted a period of rapid decline following three months of good health, but after a year Phoebe was still feeling energetic and healthy. It was too soon to tell if she'd truly beaten the cancer, but she wasn't going to wait around and find out. When she'd been diagnosed, she recorded her response as "Oh no—there are all these things I haven't yet done, and now will never have a chance to find out." When she ended up having another chance, she wasn't going to let it go to waste.

Deciding that she might as well schedule more trips as long as she was feeling well, Phoebe scaled up her travel. The year after her diagnosis, she booked trips to Peru, Suriname, and Nepal. These were not easy excursions. On the contrary, they required a series of in-country flights, three-hour journeys on canoes, and hikes into high altitude. The in-country flights were booked on unreliable airlines (the only ones available) and were frequently canceled at the last minute or delayed for long blocks of time. Many of the best birding locales consisted of

---

* Olivia Gentile notes in her extensive biography of Snetsinger that this kind of projected life span for such a diagnosis would not normally be given by most doctors now. Instead, they would provide a range of typical responses to the illness, along with the observation that results can vary.

rain forests filled with malarial mosquitoes and other unpleas-
antries. Yet before these trips were completed, Phoebe was in
such good spirits that she signed on to go to Brazil as well.

A pattern was established. Phoebe would travel to far-flung
regions and trek into forests or bogs to search for birds all day,
returning to a lodge or inn for nighttime paperwork, sometimes
by candlelight. The trips would last ten days, or two weeks, or
sometimes a full month. Gone was the idea of "a couple of big
trips each year." Adventures were scheduled in Australia and
Antarctica. At home, Phoebe would flesh out her detailed taxonomy of birds she'd seen around the world. It was a pattern, a
routine, and a way of life.

After several years of roaming the earth to see birds of
all species, Phoebe Snetsinger was a grandmaster of birding.
The numbers grew and grew. In her first few years of birding,
Phoebe had seen six hundred species of birds—but she'd now
seen nearly five thousand. In a single year of manic travel, she
saw more than one thousand new species, and then settled
into an average of five hundred species per year. She now held
the women's world record for most identified birds, but she set
her sights on the overall record. She was all-in.

All of a sudden, competition mattered. She records the
shift in her memoir: "It seemed clear that I could reach 5,000
[total sightings] during the coming year. Several male birders
had passed this mark by now, but I could be the first woman
to do it, and that idea appealed to me." Another health scare
came and went, as Phoebe was once again given a clean bill
of health after a resurgence of cancer. She was living on borrowed time, she explained to a reporter writing a newspaper
article on her quest, but she was determined to live well.

One Million Photos

Thomas Hawk has a busy day job, a wife, and four young children. As a lifelong photographer, he also has an audacious goal: to shoot and publish one million photos. As he describes it, pretty much every moment of his free time is spent taking photos, editing photos, sharing photos, or thinking about photos.

Thomas takes his camera everywhere, and he goes a lot of places. Weekends are spent flying out to the one hundred biggest cities in the United States, a project he expects to take at least a decade to complete. When he encounters people on the street asking for money, he offers them $2 in exchange for taking their photo, compiling a collection of authentic portraits of street life.

I snap plenty of photos with my phone as I wander the world, but that doesn't require much skill. For Thomas, the goal isn't just one million snapshots, it's one million *processed* and *posted* photos. He's an amateur photographer with an attention to detail that exceeds that of some professionals. To reach the million milestone, Thomas estimates it will require at least ten times as many shutter clicks. The final steps don't happen in a vacuum; every finished photo is shared online and receives thousands of views, along with much commentary from other photographers.

"What this goal means most of all for me is that I will dedicate a very large portion of my life to creating art," he told me in an email exchange from his home in San Francisco. "It means that my life will be intertwined with photography in a significant and meaningful way until I die. It's a discipline to ensure that I live my life in such a way that art will play a significant and prominent role in it."

Like Martin Luther, who nailed his famous theses to the door of the Castle Church of Wittenberg, Thomas Hawk affixed his manifesto to a website for the world to see. Here's how it begins:

We all have but a short time on this earth. As slow as time can be it is also fast, swift, furious and mighty and then it's over. Jack Kerouac is dead. Andy Warhol is dead. Garry Winogrand is dead. Lee Friedlander, Stephen Shore and William Eggleston are not dead yet, but probably will be at some point. Charles Bukowski once said that endurance was more important than truth. Charles Bukowski's now dead. When I'm not taking or processing the pictures I'm mostly thinking about the pictures.

As I discovered in visiting every country in the world, once you set a big goal it is often easier to work toward it than you first expect. In Thomas's case, he originally set out to shoot five hundred thousand images. As he worked toward the goal, he realized that one million would be a bigger challenge, yet still manageable. Thomas just doesn't quit: "When I'm tired, I keep shooting," he said, as if that explains everything.

The question that a lot of people have for Thomas is "How do you do it all? How do you make time for everything?" I wondered this, too, since I stay fairly busy myself, but not to the extent that Thomas does. Here's what he told me:

The best answer is that I don't have enough time for everything. Things suffer. I get less sleep than I should. My wife would tell you that I don't give my family enough time. I'm shooting the one hundred largest cities in America right now. I've got twenty-four or so done . . . . I'd like to have the rest finished in three years. It's a constant tug-of-war between competing interests in my life. I deal with it the best I can and try to roll with the tension as best I can.

Everywhere he goes, the one-man documentary machine known as Thomas Hawk keeps chipping away at the goal, photo by photo. The structure helps. The numbers help. And most of all, the awareness that he has to live moment by moment helps.

Hobby vs. Quest

What's the difference between a hobby and a quest? You can stop thinking about a hobby, but a quest becomes a total fascination. Playing golf on the weekends is a hobby. Setting out to play St. Andrews or lower your score is a goal. Setting out to play every course in Scotland, in a set period of time, is a quest.

Phoebe Snetsinger passed quickly through the ranks of hobbyists. The goal to see as many birds as possible and become the first woman to set a new world record was a serious commitment. Thomas Hawk, on track to create one million processed and published photos, is essentially a full-time professional—even though he has a busy day job as well.

There's an obsession factor with many quests. When you wake up at night consumed by your idea, that's when you've found a quest.

Remember the words of Kathleen Taylor, who worked with hospice patients in their final days. Once you're near the end, there's no time for bullshit. But what if you decided there's no time for bullshit—or regrets—far *in advance* of the end? What if you vow to live life the way you want right now, regardless of what stage of life you're in?

To truly live without regrets, pay attention. Ask yourself hard questions and see where they lead. Do I really want this job? Is this relationship right for me? If I could do anything, would it be what I'm doing today . . . or something different?

People who live their lives in pursuit of quests or adventures understand that they have to be deliberate about doing things that matter. Every day, Adam seeks to honor the memory of his young wife Meghan by completing the list of goals she made before dying. Every day, Thomas Hawk works on his photos whenever he can grab a few minutes.

In improv theater, you always keep the story going. No stalling or backing out allowed! How about you—what's the next chapter of your story?

Remember

Meghan always went all-in, even when she was sick. She didn't want to save anything for later.

The awareness of our own mortality can keep us focused. Eyes on the prize!

When Phoebe had a brush with death, she considered "All the things I haven't done." What's on your list?

II.
Journey

————

Chapter 5

Self-Reliance

The most courageous act is to think for yourself.
Aloud. —COCO CHANEL

Lesson: **NOT EVERYONE NEEDS TO BELIEVE**
IN YOUR DREAM, BUT YOU DO.

What does it mean to do something for yourself? To choose self-reliance or independence, to face down a fear and overcome a challenge? Ask Laura Dekker, a sixteen-year-old who sued her own government for permission to undertake a solo journey at sea after social services tried to prevent it.

Life on the water was comfortable to Laura. She was born on a yacht off the coast of New Zealand and had sailed all her life, beginning with a solo trip around the harbor at age six. Ever since she was ten years old, she was clear on her intentions, planning to become the youngest person in the world to circumnavigate the globe. There was just one challenge, and it wasn't the obvious danger of pirates, storms, or losing her way. The challenge was the Dutch government, who imposed an injunction that prevented Laura from leaving her country on her own.

After a solo trip to England and back at age thirteen, when she announced plans to begin the worldwide journey the following year, the government placed her under state guardianship.

Laura ran away to St. Martin, but was found and sent back to Holland. Finally, Laura pursued a legal case against her government and won. The journey would go on.

After all the drama at home, setting out to sea seemed anticlimactic. The court case and media attention had taken a lot out of Laura, but once she was on the water she had unlimited time. There wasn't much in the way of a schedule. She had plenty of tasks to tackle, and a big book of homeschool assignments to complete, but it's hard to be more isolated than in the middle of the ocean on a small sailboat. No doubt there would be challenges ahead, but she was now in control of her circumstances. The days stretched out before her. Her time was her own, as was her journey.

Laura never wanted to be famous. After the quest was complete, it took some work to track her down for this book. When I finally found her living back in New Zealand, we exchanged emails about why she did it. "I didn't want to be the center of attention," she wrote. "I wasn't trying to become a celebrity. I just loved the sea and I wanted to do this for myself."

Life on the Run

Bryon Powell had been ultrarunning for nearly a decade when he made an abrupt change to place the sport at the center of his life. Before quitting his job, selling his house, and relocating (all at once!), he'd run the Marathon des Sables, a seven-day, six-stage, 150-mile race in the Sahara desert in which participants carry all their food and supplies except for a group tent and water. Yet as big as that challenge was, he faced a bigger hurdle in building a community, a business, and a writing career around what had formerly just been a passion.

Bryon's motivations for change were similar to those of many other dissatisfied employees. An attorney who'd graduated from law school with honors while training for fifty-mile races, Bryon described his work as "giving technical advice on meaningless projects, and then never knowing whether the advice was even followed." He was a highly paid paper pusher with an urge to be outside and a drive to contribute to something more significant.

Out on the trail, Bryon had struck up friendships with many other athletes. These relationships were naturally oriented around races—who was going where, what the training plan was for a particular course, and so on. Outside the actual races, though, there was no single place for everyone to gather and share stories. Ultrarunners were solitary by nature, but like most people, they also craved community. Even those who had supportive families yearned for more connection with fellow enthusiasts who understood the unique challenges and benefits of training hours upon hours each weekend. Bryon had a vision to bring these people together in a virtual community that would operate in every time zone and always be available, no matter where its members happened to live. To do it right, he realized, would require an all-in commitment that drew on all his resources for a long period of time.

Flying home from Morocco, he made the decision: It was time to move forward with the plan, now or never. On his first day back, he listed his home with a real estate agent. The goal was to downsize his life at the same time he changed careers. It was scary, he said, but he focused on the worst-case scenario: "I might fail, but I'd never forgive myself if I didn't try."

Bryon didn't want to fail. In the new project he worked ten

to fourteen hours a day, seven days a week, for more than a year. He tells people that when you find something you believe in, you should put everything you've got into it. "Once you make the leap, be patient . . . very patient and persistent. Do work your butt off for a couple years if that's how long it'll take for you to get there. Easy projects aren't quests, they're holidays from real life. Any real trial will challenge you to the core. Acknowledge that and fight like hell to keep working through it!"

"Fighting like hell" was a good attitude that well represented the spirit of a man who'd run more than one hundred miles in a single day, but it was also hard to sustain in his new role. On the road to cover a race one day, Bryon realized he'd forgotten a tripod at home. It shouldn't have been a huge deal—he was only half an hour away when he made the discovery—but he nearly had a nervous breakdown. "I wanted to quit right then," he says, recalling the weight of the past year hitting him at the gas station where he was refueling the car. Thinking over his strong reaction, he realized he just needed to pace himself better. He could still work hard, but he had to learn to work smarter.

Bryon recovered, took a break to resettle, then returned his focus to the worldwide community he'd chosen to serve for at least five years.

Embracing Rejection

If you're trying to do something new, you may feel uncomfortable with the idea of starting, or you may worry that your idea won't be accepted by everyone. One way to "get over it" is to learn to become comfortable with failure. Jason Comely created a real-life game called Rejection Therapy that encourages players to engage in social experiments. The goal of the game is to ask for something and have the request denied, stretching your comfort zone.* If you ask for something and get it, that's a bonus—but the day's round of Rejection Therapy isn't over, because you ultimately have to be rejected before moving on. Since beginning the game, Jason has seen fans and adherents practice it to become more bold in making requests.

Perhaps the most ambitious rejection project has been thirty-year-old Jia Jiang's in Austin, Texas. Prior to beginning the project, Jia (pronounced "Zhaw") had been turned down in an investment pitch for a business he was trying to start. The rejection stung, and he wanted to desensitize himself against similar pain in the future. Having heard of Jason's Rejection Therapy concept, Jia decided to embrace it with a twist. He'd launch a "100 days of public rejection" project where he'd make a series of bold requests from strangers and record the results.

Jia recorded his requests on a camera phone and uploaded them to YouTube, creating a built-in accountability effect. Once he started, he couldn't stop—he knew he'd be letting people down. He began with tasks that were relatively simple: for example, asking to deliver pizza for Domino's, or asking for a "burger refill" at a fast-food chain.

One of his first requests became a popular online hit. Jia visited a Krispy Kreme donut shop and requested a box of do-nuts in the shape of Olympic rings. To his surprise, the cashier took his request seriously. "How are they linked?" she asked. "I didn't pay much attention to the Olympics this year."

Jackie, the cashier, pulled out a sheet of receipt paper and

---

* Jason: "Your comfort zone may be more like a cage you can't escape from than a safe place you can retreat to."

began sketching an idea. "How about red, yellow, blue, green, and white? Do you think that looks right?"

At this point Jia was wondering if he should have picked a different experiment, but he dutifully sat down and waited for Jackie to return with the box. When she did, with the donuts linked in the shape of the Olympic rings, she had another surprise. "How do I pay?" Jia asked.

"Don't worry about it," Jackie said. "This one's on us."*

Jia's requests got crazier and more elaborate as he went along. He visited the Austin Humane Society and asked to borrow a dog for an outing. "I want to make him the happiest dog in the world for a day!" he told the representative, who was polite but firm in declining to loan out a dog for an afternoon romp through the park. He went to a fire station and asked if he could slide down a fire pole, and he asked a police officer if he could sit in his cop car. By day fifteen, Jia was cruising along with his rejection project, picking up suggestions from people who watched his videos and from strangers he encountered through practicing rejection.

Whether his request succeeded or failed, Jia extracted a lesson from each experience. He asked a stranger to "partner up" on buying a lottery ticket, and upon analyzing the interaction noted that there are many hidden costs of such an exchange. Another day he visited a BBQ place in Austin and asked to grill his own meat. The guy on the front line thought it was hilarious, but the manager said no—producing the lesson that it's important to funnel your requests through the right gatekeeper. (File under: "I fight authority, authority always wins.")

---

* "My faith in humanity is restored!" wrote a commenter who saw the video. "I hope she got promoted," someone else said.

Jia learned that rejection, like experience, produces confidence. The act of moving forward, continuing to make requests despite a number of failures, was empowering.

What Does Self-Reliance Mean to You?

I asked this open-ended question to readers from several different countries. Here are a few of their answers.

Knowing that I can rely on myself to take care of things.
—*@AvalonMel*

The belief that I am responsible for my achievements and failures, that I first look for solutions to problems within myself. —*@JackPenner*

The ability to love yourself and to know, no matter what, you'll be OK. The ability to wear silence like an old shoe.
—*@QCTravelWriter*

It's my path, not yours. —*@BSoist*

Knowing yourself and having purpose. —*@MichelleDavella*

That I can get myself out of most any situation and live life on my own terms. —*@CC_Chapman*

The combination of self-reliance and independence gives me autonomy. "Need to do" is defined by me, not by someone telling me. —*@SethGetz*

Self-reliance: Learn when you're stuck. Independence: Learn at your own convenience. —*@ParthPareek*

Trusting yourself to do what you say you're going to do. If you can't rely on yourself, no one else can.
—*@PhotoMktMentor*

"If I Didn't Do It, I Would Always Wonder"

What's it like to be blind? According to Julie Johnson, the average sighted person has no idea. Perhaps you've played a game where you closed your eyes and tried to find your way to the bathroom down the hall. Maybe you bumped into a wall or became frightened and gave up, thinking to yourself that you could never manage not having the ability to see. As Julie put it, "blind people get a lot of practice at being blind." It's hard in the beginning—there's a lot of stuff to learn, from reading Braille to learning to tell when your food is cooked properly, and countless other details. It takes time to acquire these skills, much longer than the brief experiment of trying to walk down the hall to the bathroom. But then, because you get a lot of practice at being blind, you learn. You improve, and most of the time, blind people can become largely self-reliant.

Julie was born with glaucoma, a degenerative eye disease that often leads to blindness. When she needed a guide dog, she first looked to the many different programs that train service animals—but then she decided to make her own plan. Some of the guide dog schools retain ownership of the dog and train them using corrective-based methods. In all her work with animals, Julie had come to favor a less corrective-based approach, so she decided to do it herself. For her, at least part of the motivation came from so many people dismissing the idea offhand.

"There were a lot of people telling me that it couldn't be done," she said. "They told me it was dangerous, that I was crazy, that there was no need when there were charities that would provide me with a trained guide dog. The more people tried to push me away, the more I became intrigued with the idea. I kept thinking, *Why not?* I knew it would be tough and I knew there would be setbacks, but I truly felt like I could do it."

Julie didn't become legally blind until age twenty, and she'd worked with dogs as a young adult. Even if it *was* hard, she had to do it. "I needed to do this Big Thing," she said. "I didn't know then that it was a Big Thing. I just felt drawn to this path. I knew it was something that I needed to do for myself. If I didn't do it, I would always wonder about what could have been."

❂

This last statement, "If I didn't do it, I would always wonder about what could have been," was repeated over and over and in many different ways by the people I talked with. I understood it well, because it's exactly how I felt when I first began to ponder the goal of traveling to every country. I had to do it! It was such a ridiculous idea that I knew I'd always wonder about it if I didn't try.

For someone who has visited every country in the world, I have a terrible sense of direction. I'm not legally blind like Julie, but almost everywhere I go I get lost at least once—and this includes my own city, which is conveniently laid out on a grid. Yet even with my constant ability to forget which way I turned, I love heading out for a long run in a new country without a map or phone. There's a thrill that comes from doing something that feels new and disorienting, and the times when I've run on the treadmill in a hotel gym, or simply back and forth on a street in sight of my guesthouse, just don't feel the same. It's all about the feeling of being out there on your own, relying on yourself to run ten miles or more in an unfamiliar city and still make it back for happy hour.*

You Must Believe

As I talked with the young sailor Laura and many others, I was struck by an important principle: You must believe that your quest can be successful, even if no one else does. You can deal with setbacks, misadventures, and even disasters as long as you still believe you can overcome the hardships and see your way to the end.

If no one else believes, it may be hard—but you can still do it.

Out on the high seas, Laura struggled with many things, battling loneliness and the Dutch social services—but she never doubted her ability to complete the journey. Whatever your quest, you, too, must believe.

In Laura's case, the dream of self-reliance meant spending 518 days at sea. For Bryon, it meant leaving a stable career to build a community around his passion of ultrarunning. For Julie, it meant training her own guide dog.

A desire for ownership and accomplishment, the fierce desire for control over one's life—these are powerful forces. Being told you can't do something is supremely motivating. There is joy in the retelling of the stories. At one point in my research I talked with someone who ran fifty marathons in a year. "According to conventional wisdom," he said, "You're just

---

* Free training tip: If you're trying to run progressively longer distances, all you need to do is run halfway in one direction. One way or another, you have to get back!

not supposed to run a marathon every week. But that's why it's so satisfying!"

In South Korea I served on a panel with a man who became an entrepreneur at age sixteen. For the next fifteen years he built a series of businesses with many employees. "People laughed at me," he said through a translator. "But they're not laughing now."

Whatever your quest, you must believe!

Life Is Risky

Laura continued her journey from shore to shore, eventually logging more than a year at sea before completing the quest as planned. She and I exchanged emails while I was traveling through Asia and she was in her new home in New Zealand, where she was studying to earn her divemaster license. She told me that her greatest challenge was overcoming the objections of her own government in allowing her to pursue the journey. She was also surprised by all the people who chimed in with negative comments after her legal case received worldwide attention. As a result of Laura's journey, Guinness World Records stopped publishing the achievements of the world's youngest sailors.

Laura's dad was supportive, but plenty of other people weren't. As she wrote me, "I know about sailing. I know what to do if a storm breaks. But people are a mystery that is a lot harder to deal with than high seas."

She complained about what she saw as the Dutch government's overbearing attitude in their attempt to legally prevent her from sailing the world as a teenager. In their defense, however, a spokesperson from the Netherlands Bureau for Youth Care noted that if her journey was unsuccessful—especially if she was harmed or killed en route—people would have complained about her being allowed to leave with no legal challenge. "If Laura had drowned," he said, "we would be accused of not doing enough to protect her. Thank God she's OK and I think that's partly due to the safety measures we enforced as part of the condition for allowing her to go."

❂

I live in Oregon, near good running trails and mountain climbs that are attempted by thousands of people each year. Some of these climbs are tough, but almost all are completed without harm coming to anyone.

On one recent weekend, however, tragedy struck as three hikers were killed in an unusual accident. Despite the fact that all the climbers were experienced and had left for the hike when weather conditions were good, some observers blamed the accident on "risky behavior" and suggested various reforms that wouldn't have made any difference in this case.

Both of these responses—to Laura's journey and to the Oregon tragedy—are based on the outcome of the situation. The outside world judges our actions based almost entirely on results—even though the results aren't always up to us.

When I visited the Iranian territory of Kish Island, I came in on a flight from Dubai. Almost everyone else on the plane was a migrant worker seeking to renew their eligibility for work in Dubai. I was the only Westerner, and the supervisor pulled me out of the immigration line and into a small office. "Wait here," he said, then disappeared with my passport for at least twenty minutes.

I began to worry. Even though Kish Island is a visa-free zone, meaning that anyone should be able to visit, at the time relations between Iran and the United States were terribly strained. While I was there, three other Americans were imprisoned on the Iranian mainland on charges of trespassing even as their families denied any offense.

The supervisor came back with another official. "Fingerprints," the new official said matter-of-factly as he produced an ink pad. I kept smiling and made vague remarks about how excited I was to visit Kish Island. He asked a few questions about my occupation, another tricky topic since I didn't want to mention I was a writer. (In many countries, "writer" means "journalist," and journalists are treated with suspicion in places without a free press.)

I told him I was a small-business owner and publisher, a true statement that also seemed generic enough to avoid further questioning. Finally he said the magic words: "OK, here is your passport. Permission has been granted to enter."

I'd made it to Iran! Just as important, I made it out safely when the time came to return to Dubai. But what if I hadn't? What if I'd been detained or even imprisoned, like those three other Americans? I have no doubt that some of my friends and readers around the world would have been concerned and saddened. But I'm also pretty sure that others would have said, "What was he thinking? That was stupid!"

Sailing the world alone, climbing mountains, or visiting Iran as a citizen of the country that the Iranian government calls "the great Satan" all involve risks. In the end these pursuits will be judged on the outcome. Consider it like this:

WHAT PEOPLE SAY ABOUT AN ADVENTURE OR QUEST
  THAT INVOLVES PERCEIVED RISK:
Successful Outcome: brave, courageous, confident
Failed Outcome: stupid, risky, naive, arrogant

Judgments about whether a quest is brave or stupid tend to be relative. While authorities *can* play a role in setting conditions for a quest that serve to protect the fearless from themselves, ultimately assessments of a quest's worthiness depend on the result. Sometimes life itself is risky. There are few goals worth pursuing that are totally risk free.

❂

Chris McCandless gained fame and notoriety for his attempt to live off the land in Alaska—an attempt that ultimately led to his untimely death. But McCandless wasn't trying to be famous, and he didn't plan on dying. He was searching within himself for something that was hard to define. Before his death, he wrote a letter that was later quoted by Jon Krakauer in the book *Into the Wild.* The excerpt below has inspired many people to rethink their lives and routines.

> *I'd like to repeat the advice that I gave you before, in that I think you really should make a radical change in your lifestyle and begin to boldly do things which you may previously never have thought of doing, or been too hesitant to attempt. So many people live within unhappy circumstances and yet will not take the initiative to change their situation because they are conditioned to a life of security,*

conformity, and conservatism, all of which may appear to give one peace of mind, but in reality nothing is more damaging to the adventurous spirit within a man than a secure future. The very basic core of a man's living spirit is his passion for adventure. The joy of life comes from our encounters with new experiences, and hence there is no greater joy than to have an endlessly changing horizon, for each day to have a new and different sun.

The cause of McCandless's death remained unknown for years afterward. In *Into the Wild*, Krakauer speculated that he'd died from slow poisoning after eating toxic potato seeds. This theory was criticized on the grounds that the seeds weren't poisonous, and the commonly accepted premise that McCandless had intended to commit suicide. Krakauer felt strongly that this wasn't the case—McCandless "wanted to test himself, not to kill himself," he said—but for more than fifteen years he didn't have proof.

Proof arrived in the form of new evidence. Another writer, working with a lab at Indiana University, surmised that the potato seeds in question weren't always toxic, but for someone who was weak and emaciated, they would be. Krakauer had this hypothesis checked with independent labs that tested the same kinds of seeds that Chris McCandless had recorded eating in his journal. The hypothesis was confirmed and the mystery solved: McCandless made a mistake when he ate the wrong seeds, but he wasn't reckless and self-destructive as the critics had claimed.

It was a risk for Bryon to quit his job and pursue a new career focused on ultrarunning, a sport not known for its lucrative commercialization. But Bryon knew that the real risk was to stay in one place. He chose the safe path, the one that led to the trail and nearly one hundred races each year.

Jia learned to take small risks every day by asking restaurants if he could cook his own meals and asking police officers if he could sit in their cruisers. At first it was hard to make even these small requests, but he grew to enjoy it as he went along.

It was an even bigger risk for Laura to sail solo around the world, relying on her own judgment to handle the difficult conditions that were nearly certain to arrive. But as she said, she had to do it for herself. After the epic journey was complete, she moved to New Zealand, the land of her birth, and began studying for her divemaster license. After spending most of her life on the water, she wasn't ready to change.

Remember

You have to believe in your quest even if others don't.

We tend to judge risk based on outcome—but the outcome isn't always up to us.

Life itself is risky. Choose your own risk level.

Chapter 6

Everyday Adventure

Do one thing every day that scares you.
—ELEANOR ROOSEVELT

Lesson: YOU CAN HAVE THE LIFE YOU WANT
NO MATTER WHO YOU ARE.

What if you're not ready to take seventeen years off and walk everywhere? Not up for running hundreds of marathons in a single year, or sailing across the ocean on your own?

Relax. Or don't relax, because a quest is rarely about taking it easy. It's about challenging yourself however you can, learning new things and exploring horizons outside your environment . . . even if you never leave home.

You can do this no matter where you live and no matter how old you are. If you want to make every day an adventure, all you have to do is prioritize adventure. It has to become more important than routine.

Every Country, Prepared on Your Plate

Tulsa, Oklahoma, isn't exactly known as a mecca for gastronomy. When I came through on a book tour, I had a hard time finding a restaurant that wasn't part of a big American chain. Ordering coffee at the bookstore café, I had to explain the difference between whole milk and skim milk to the barista . . . and then she charged me extra to substitute my preference.

Yet underneath the highway exit surface of Outback Steakhouse, Taco Bell, and your choice of hamburger joints, there are a lot of different people living in Tulsa. Like most other U.S. cities, Tulsa is becoming more diverse. Significant populations from more than fifty countries now call the area home, including immigrants from such faraway locales as Burma, China, and the Pacific Islands. The oil industry, long Tulsa's most reliable means of employment, has shifted to accommodate several aerospace and financial firms that have set up shop. The result is a diverse influx of workers from the rest of the country and overseas.

At the same time that the city was slowly enriching its demography, thirty-three-year-old Sasha Martin was changing some long-ingrained habits in her family. Three years earlier, she'd been like many others searching for a focus before settling on a quest. Her daughter Ava was six months old, and Sasha felt firmly entrenched in Oklahoma life—perhaps too much so.

Sasha had grown up overseas with a foster parent who was stationed in Europe as a financial director. When she was younger, it was no big deal to hop over to Greece for a weekend, or to visit Scandinavia on holiday. Now that she was living in Oklahoma with a child of her own, the opportunities to see the world were much more limited.

The Big Idea she settled on was to embrace culture through cuisine. "Stovetop Travel" was Sasha's project to introduce meals from around the world into her home kitchen. If it sounds simple, understand that this was no "buy a wok and learn to make stir-fry" weeklong task. Sasha had earned a culinary arts degree after returning to the United States as a young adult, and she was determined to put her education to work. The cooking project would last nearly four years and be truly global. Every good goal has a deadline (Pay attention: This is a recurring theme of many stories), and Sasha chose to cook an entire meal from each country's cuisine every week, following the alphabet in A–Z fashion for a total of 195 weeks.*

She began with Afghanistan, steaming up basmati rice and learning how to make *sabse borani,* a spinach and yogurt dip. Next was Albania, featuring dishes such as *turli perimesh,* a selection of mixed vegetables. For each week's meal, Sasha conducted detailed research, checking cookbooks and online recipes, and consulting a growing group of online friends who followed her progress as she moved from Angola through Brunei. Each meal was complete, with at least one main course (sometimes several) and a generous serving of starters and side dishes. Whenever possible, Sasha would play music from the country she was featuring, and invite friends to join the dinner.

How did this go over at home? Well, it took some time. At first, Sasha's husband, Keith, wasn't thrilled about the idea. A self-described picky eater, Keith would have been happy eating hamburgers and french fries every day for the rest of his life. Before meeting Sasha, he'd never seen an eggplant or tried fresh spinach.

---

*Astute readers may note that Sasha, in planning to cook a meal from every country, has two more countries on her target list than exist on the list I used for my round-the-world tour. That's because she includes the Republic of Taiwan and Kosovo on her list. Neither are UN member states, but I've been to both.

Fortunately, Keith agreed to be supportive, and even helped document the process through photography. As one week's menu gave way to the next and Ava grew, he created a regular video feature in which he filmed her impressions of each country's food.

After Sasha finished the "A" countries (Afghanistan, Albania, Algeria, Andorra, Angola, and so forth) and moved on to the Bs, she was sitting one day at her dining room table, thumbing through cookbooks in search of what to make for Bulgaria. A knock sounded at the door, and a young man appeared who was selling children's books for a summer job. The young man had an accent and happened to be from Bulgaria. Sasha invited him in and quizzed him on the recipes she was studying. (To thank him, she bought a book before he left.)

A similar thing happened with Finland. Sasha was at a children's play group and met a Finnish woman who ended up following her home to help make *pulla,* a sweet bread made with cardamom and raisins.

When she started the project, Sasha's initial motivations were to improve the family's diet and get out of a rut. Missing the travel experiences of her youth, she hoped to rekindle a sense of foreign connection by dicing peppers and baking pastries. But the message ran deeper. Sasha longed to facilitate a peace offering of people breaking bread together and understanding different cultures.

Three years into the project, her vision had expanded. She was asked to give talks at schools and other forums. Her project was being replicated elsewhere, by other families who embraced the idea of learning to understand culture through food. In fact, she was preparing for a collective dining experience called the Two-Hundred-Foot Table. "I expected the adventure to change our eating habits," Sasha wrote me in an email, "but I didn't expect it to affect all other aspects of my life the way it has."

Meanwhile, Ava's first solid food was Afghan chicken. By three years old, she was equally comfortable using silverware or chopsticks. Before her fifth birthday she will have tried food from every country in the world.

The Recipe for an Everyday Quest

I liked Sasha's story because it illustrates adventure and in-genuity. She drew on a love for foreign travel and added in her degree in culinary arts. Not only that, but she didn't just decide to "cook a bunch of different meals"—she made it a quest, with a clear goal and a defined set of milestones.

What was special about Sasha's cooking project? Why couldn't she just "make foreign food" once in a while, instead of taking on the task of preparing unique meals from every country?

Sasha's project was bigger *because* it was a quest. She chose something specific to work on over time—an endeavor that was fun, challenging, and meaningful. Recall the characteristics of quests that we examined earlier:

A clear goal. In the case of Sasha's project (and mine!), there are a set, limited number of countries. I planned to visit each, and Sasha planned to research and prepare a full meal from each. It would be a lot of work, but both of us knew what we were working toward and how success would be defined.

Measurable progress. Sasha and her family were able to see how far along they were each week. In addition to conducting a countdown, every week they'd color in another country on a map that hung in the dining room. Even though they weren't hurrying things along, it was fun to see how far they'd come. They could also look ahead to future country "visits," something that created anticipation for each week's meal.

A sense of calling or mission. Sasha deployed her culinary skills for a purpose that went beyond making a red wine reduction or knowing the difference between sweet potatoes and yams. The whole point was to be a part of the world beyond Oklahoma. Yearning for the life she had known as a child, she found a way to bring it to the table. Later, the vision expanded: She began speaking in classrooms and community centers. The goal was to spread a message of peace through understanding different cultures.

Sacrifice . . . or at least effort. Did Sasha's quest require sacrifice? Perhaps not—at least as long as you don't count the adjustments that Keith went through as he learned to expand his palate. But it certainly involved concentrated effort over time. Having chosen to follow an A–Z country-by-country order, Sasha couldn't mix it up too much. If she entered a rut or encountered a series of countries that were hard to plan for, she had to figure it out. No excuses!

Other Everyday Adventures

In researching this book, I heard from people who'd undertaken all sorts of quests like Sasha's—visiting, either figuratively or literally, a large number of locations. Marc Ankenbauer, a self-proclaimed "Glacial Explorer," devoted nearly ten years to jumping into every lake in the Glacier and Waterton Lakes National Parks. These parks contain 168 lakes in total, many requiring off-trail hiking through dense vegetation and rough mountainous terrain to reach, and including land on both sides of the U.S.–Canada border. Marc had the idea to challenge his fitness level and raise money for Camp Mak-A-Dream, a charity that offers free outdoor experiences for children and teens living with cancer.

A couple of my other favorite projects in this broad category involved tracking down special buildings through a series of field trips that increased in distance as the project developed.

Case Number One: Every Basilica

A former atheist, Allie Terrell converted to Catholicism at the age of twenty-three after reading a book by C. S. Lewis. When Allie was looking for a church to attend, a Google search directed her to a *basilica*—a word she'd heard before but wasn't entirely familiar with. Further research revealed that a basilica was a special kind of church building, and at the time there were sixty-eight in the United States.

Allie was interested in why some churches had received special status. There was a church on every corner in her home state of Wisconsin, but you had to go out of your way to find a basilica. After visiting one, Allie and her boyfriend Jason were intrigued. Basilicas tended to have special architectural features, often maintaining a sense of unity with earlier church building design but other times giving a nod to contemporary style. Some were particularly beautiful, and others had become pilgrimage sites for historical reasons. Allie and Jason decided to turn it into a project: They'd visit every basilica in the United States, telling the story along the way.

Allie is a computer scientist by day, and naturally skilled with managing information. Most of these historical buildings have very little online documentation. Many Catholics don't even know what a basilica is, and the elderly caretakers of the buildings tend not to spend their time editing *Wikipedia* articles. When Jason and Allie noticed this knowledge gap, they decided to fill it by documenting their experiences through photography and narratives.

The quest has expanded geographically to the point that they are now starting to travel further from their home base in Wisconsin. One challenge: The number of basilicas increases over time as church leaders bestow the special status on more buildings. Allie and Jason plan to deal with this obstacle by "freezing the design" at some point and focusing on the ones that have been recognized as of that moment.

Case Number Two: Every Baseball Stadium

At the age of five, Josh Jackson participated in a ritual familiar to many children. His dad took him to a big sports stadium for the first time. In Josh's case, the stadium was the Houston Astrodome, and the game was Major League Baseball. Perhaps it was the sense of experiencing an important rite of passage, or maybe it was just the box of Cracker Jacks that came with a free prize at the bottom, but whatever it was, Josh was enthralled.

For the rest of his childhood, then continuing fifteen years into adulthood, Josh and his dad have been trying to visit every Major League stadium in the United States and Canada. In the early days, they saved money by packing peanut-butter-and-jelly sandwiches for meals and sleeping in the back of a Ford Econo-line van while on trips to faraway stadiums in the Midwest.

Josh wrote to me about the magic of walking into a big stadium for the first time, emerging from the top of a tunnel and into an instant community of fellow sports fans: "I wanted to experience that glorious walk in every other stadium. There's still nothing quite like that walk, when you enter into a tunnel and come out into a new stadium for the first time, seeing the players running drills and the stands filling with people."

After that first visit, Josh and his dad began to take regular road trips. One summer, his dad sprung a surprise. "How about we go to . . . New York City?" he said with a smile. Josh was thrilled, but that wasn't the surprise.

"How do you think we should get there?" his dad continued. Josh was confused. "Um, in the car?"

That's when his dad dropped the real surprise with another smile. "How about we hitchhike?"

Josh told me the rest of the story in an email:

A few months later my mother and three sisters dropped us off at a truck stop a few miles from our house and few hours later we were on our way. All said and done, we hitchhiked 1,300 miles over the course of ten days. We received twenty-two rides in total and our journey took us from West Michigan to see games in Pittsburgh, New York, Baltimore and Philadelphia. The most memorable ride was in the back of a pick-up truck, my dad and I sitting on either side of a Harley Davidson, from Eastern Pennsylvania straight into New York City via the George Washington Bridge. Spending time with my dad—watching him lead us, watching him interact with others through conversations in the hot sun and on Interstate ramps, making signs and experiencing the freedom and fear of hitchhiking—these moments . . . were certainly the most meaningful to me.

Walking into the Astrodome had initiated a love of baseball, and hitchhiking to New York City cemented the idea that this would be a lifelong project. As Josh grew up, he planned to see a game in every Major League Baseball stadium. It's been an on-again, off-again project for much of his life, and he now has just a few remaining stadiums to hit.

Life as an Experiment in Bravery

I first learned the concept of *life experiments* from Allan Bacon several years ago. Allan was a normal guy with a good life and a great family, but he felt a vague sense of discontent—much like many other people I hear from. Allan couldn't abandon it all and move to a life of backpacking around the world, and he wasn't keen on running a marathon every Sunday. But he began changing his routine however he could, on the theory that even a small degree of change would be beneficial. Since he began his initial life experiments, which were as simple as visiting the art museum on his lunch break or taking a photography class, he's been much happier.

In a short book, *The Flinch*, Julien Smith wrote about his own series of life experiments, challenging readers to give some a try. One of my favorite passages involves a deliberate act of household destruction:

> Go to the kitchen and grab a mug you don't like. Mug in hand, go to a place in your house with a hard floor. Hold the mug in front of you, in your outstretched hand. Say good-bye to it. Now, drop the cup. Whatever rationalization you're using right now is a weak spot for you. Flag it. You'll see it again and again. Drop the damn cup. Did you do it? If so, you'll notice one thing: breaking your programming requires a single moment of strength.

Aside from smashing mugs in your kitchen, what other kinds of life experiments can shake things up for the better? Here's a quick list of possibilities.

- Attempt to begin a conversation with a stranger.
- Take only cold showers for a week.
- Sit in a public place and stare straight ahead for ten minutes.
- Make a rule that you'll reach for your gym clothes as soon as the alarm goes off (no snooze button!).
- Go to work a different way or by a different form of transportation.
- Completely rearrange the furniture in your living room or bedroom.
- Vary a workout routine by choosing exercises based on dice rolls.

- Join a free foreign language meetup (visit Meetup.com and search for your choice of language).
- Offer a room of your house for rent on Airbnb.com.
- Offer your couch to a traveler on Couchsurfing.com.
- In a recurring meeting, deliberately choose a different seat.
- If you're usually active in meetings, determine to speak less. If you're usually silent, speak up!
- Post "Anything I can help you with?" on Facebook, Twitter, or wherever you gather with friends online. Respond to as many answers as you can.
- Laugh out loud in public at something that isn't funny. See what happens.
- Bring dog treats to the park and give them to strangers (primarily the ones who have dogs).
- Stop carrying an umbrella when it rains. You might get wet, but chances are you won't melt.

Some of these ideas may seem silly or irrelevant. Focus on the ones that are interesting, and if you *still* don't find any, create your own.

Should You Document Your Quest?

Yes, probably, in some fashion. But how? Some people I talked with said that they wished they'd been more attentive to documenting their journey, others happily chronicled *everything*, and a third group was happy to pursue their project without keeping track of all the details.

Josh Jackson, who has visited almost every baseball stadium in the United States, says that his biggest disappointment is that he didn't pay more attention to recording the experience. He wishes he'd taken more pictures and kept the ticket stubs, and there's no way to correct that now since those stadium visits are long in the past. Allie Terrell, who is hoping to visit every basilica, told me that she wished she had improved her photography skills before getting too far into the quest. "I'd love to have a complete collection of basilica photos when I'm done," she said, "But I may need to revisit some of the sites, since my early work leaves something to be desired."

Options for documentation include:

- Photography or videography
- Writing or blogging
- Collecting souvenirs or mementos (like Josh's ticket stubs)
- Keeping a scrapbook (either a traditional one or a digital one)
- Something different

It's helpful to decide what form of documentation, if any, best suits your preferences. When I first started traveling I took a camera everywhere and dutifully attempted to take photos. I wasn't very good at photography, and I didn't always enjoy it. In fact, sometimes I even found it stressful—I realized I was spending a lot of time looking for something that would make a good picture, instead of actually enjoying my surroundings. I finally stopped taking pictures except for snapshots on my phone, and I felt relieved. I continued writing, a form of documentation that made more sense to me.

Lesson: Complete the kind of recording that makes sense to you, not what you feel you *should* do. A few helpful resources for documentation are available at FindtheQuest.com.

Everyone Is Busy

Are you busy? Join the club. Everyone is busy, yet we all have access to the same amount of time. If you want to prioritize adventure but can't find the time, something's got to give.

Sasha Martin found a way to bring the world to her dining room table in Tulsa, Oklahoma. Others found different ways to create adventure, changing their routines and bringing greater challenge into their lives.

There are two popular theories of change making:

1. Make small and incremental (but regular) changes. Mix it up.

2. Do it all at once. Quit smoking immediately. Take cold showers. Enter boot camp for the soul—whatever you need to do, don't wait.

Either of these options can work, but there's no third theory of waiting for change to knock on your door and announce its arrival. You must do *something*. The sooner, the better.

Remember

If you're not ready to run 250 marathons in a year, you can still pursue a quest.

Don't just do something "fun." Find a way to create structure around a project and build in a timeline.

Connect your skills and interests with an extended challenge—such as visiting every basilica, or cooking nearly two hundred unique meals.

ROUTINE

The quest helped to orient me. I loved travel, even aimless travel with no set goal, but attaching it to something of greater significance gave it more weight. The quest offered a measurable objective and a series of progressive steps I could follow. Even though it was ultimately more about the journey than the eventual destination, having a destination in mind provided an anchor.

A typical two-week trip took me completely around the world, or to at least two major regions outside of North America. I'd plan the next trip as soon as I returned home, immediately sending off my passport to another embassy or visa service to receive the necessary approval. Often I had multiple round-the-world tickets in motion at the same time, switching back and forth as I arrived in worldwide hub cities before heading out to more remote locations. If it sounds confusing, it was.

When I had trouble getting somewhere, I'd reroute the trip in real time, finding another country to visit and saving the troublesome one for later. Many of the visa applications came down to the wire, with my passport being released just in time for the visa service to pick it up in Washington and FedEx it to me the day before my departure. More than once I'd fly to Chicago or New York, where I planned to connect to an international flight, and await the arrival of my passport at a hotel with fingers crossed. A friend christened this the "Guillebeau Rule of Visa Applications"—you'll usually get the visa you need, but not until the last minute.

With all this travel, where did I fit in? Where was home? I was American, with an apartment in Oregon and a passport with a blue seal, but I didn't feel especially patriotic. Coming back sometimes felt like going on another trip. Yet I was perceived as a stranger in many of the countries I visited; I was usually treated well or at least with curiosity, but always as someone foreign.

Where I truly felt at home, I learned as I went along, was on the road itself. Heading to another stop, navigating another bus system, or queuing up for another second-class overnight train ticket—these were the activities that felt normal. The road was the routine, and the quest became a comfort.

I learned to pack the same things for every trip. Simple clothes that could layer. At least one nice shirt. Always the running shoes, if for no other reason than to inspire me to action out of guilt for lugging them so far around the planet.

❂

Sri Lanka was my one-hundredth country. I'd been looking forward to the visit for several months, since I saw it both as a place I'd long wanted to experience and as a symbolic victory that marked the more-than-halfway point of my goal. I touched down in the capital city of Colombo on a cramped redeye from Qatar, arriving at dawn. Immigration and the busy morning traffic took a while, so when I finally made it to the hotel around noon, I was glad to hear they had a room for me.

I dropped off my bags and took a quick walk around town. Then I laid down for a nap.

Lesson: Be careful about short naps after changing six time zones and not sleeping the night before. My power nap turned into a full-on sleep cycle. When I woke up eight hours later, my first thought was "Wow, it gets dark early here!" Then I saw the alarm clock and realized what had happened. After sleeping through the entire afternoon and evening, I knew I'd be up for the rest of the night.

It turned out that staying up all night in Colombo was surprisingly fun. I had a balcony in my room that overlooked a beach, directly next to the main downtown area. At the time of my visit Sri Lanka was engulfed in a longstanding civil war. The capital city was safe, but foreigners were discouraged from traveling farther out. Soldiers stood watch on every street corner.

I wandered out onto the beach, waving to the soldiers and a group of children who were still out playing soccer despite the late hour. I walked back and forth along the sand under a high moon, watching the waves rush in and out. "One hundred countries!" I said out loud. So far, so fast, yet still so much further to go.

Back in the hotel I got comfortable and set up a mobile office for the night. I was working on an overdue writing project, and I decided there was no time like the present to knock it out. Breakfast was at least six hours away. I boiled water for Nescafé and settled in, drafting my pages and pacing the room for a break every hour.

As the sun peeked through the clouds I was almost done.

First in line at the restaurant, I ordered two plates of food and more coffee.

What a crazy life, *I thought.* Here I am in Sri Lanka, watching the sunrise after staying up all night in my one-hundredth country. *Yet it all felt normal.*

A couple of days later, my sleep cycle having never really adjusted, I boarded a Cathay Pacific flight to Hong Kong. Many more countries lay ahead, and I was eager to keep going.

Strange as it was, this was my new routine.

Chapter 7

Time and Money

*All artists are willing to suffer for their work. But why
are so few prepared to learn to draw?*   —BANKSY

Lesson: BEFORE BEGINNING A QUEST,
COUNT THE COST.

I first met twenty-one-year-old Nate Damm in Portland,
Maine. A group of us were sitting at an outdoor café, and
Nate was the quiet guy in a corner, paying attention but not
saying much. After everyone else had talked for a while, a mutual friend caught my eye and pointed to Nate. "You should
hear what this guy is doing next year," he said.

Nate looked pained at being the center of attention, but
then explained that he was planning to walk across the entire
United States, from Maine to San Francisco. He was so quiet
that I had to ask him to repeat himself. "You're doing what?"

He told me again, matter-of-factly, that he'd arranged to
leave Maine the following spring and walk all the way to the
West Coast over the next six or seven months. Everyone at
the table had questions—ones you could tell he'd heard many
times before.

"Really, you're walking across America?"

"Yes."

"Why?"

"I just feel like I should. I've had this idea for two years and it won't go away."

"How?"

"Backpack, walking shoes, sleeping bag."

I went away impressed, but also wondering if he would actually do it. The walking path that Nate had chosen spanned more than three thousand miles and crossed several different climates, including an extended stretch through the Mojave and Great Basin Deserts in Nevada.

Nate was committed, though. As soon as the New England weather warmed after a cold winter, he packed up everything he could carry in a backpack and hit the road. From Maine he marched down through Pennsylvania and out toward the Great Lakes region. The first day was exciting ("I'm on the road!") and the second was tiring ("My feet aren't used to this."). After a while, routine set in and his muscles adjusted to regular days of walking six hours or more.

Still in the early weeks of the trip, he had a tough moment in West Virginia after a particularly hard day. Nothing had worked as he hoped—he was worn down, feeling especially alone, and a rainstorm that had started in the morning continued nonstop through the afternoon. On the verge of a physical and mental breakdown, he forced himself to back up and think about why he was doing the walk. The self-reflection helped: He realized that even though there would be plenty of hard days like this one, he valued the overall experience enough to persevere. His courage and stamina restored, he crossed the state line and kept going.

After growing accustomed to the pattern of daily progress,

albeit sometimes in the rain, Nate settled into life in the slow-but-steady lane. Every day he'd get up and walk. Sometimes he'd meet people along the way. Truck drivers stopped to pass him water (and once in a while, beer). Strangers invited him into their homes for dinner. Other days, he would be on his own the whole day, putting mile after mile on his canvas hiking boots as he slogged through the Midwest and kept moving toward California. Either way, the task was the same: putting one foot in front of the other, literally.

❂

My favorite part of talking with Nate after his trip was when I asked him about the struggles he encountered. "Walking across the country sounds like a crazy and unimaginable idea to most people," he told me. "But once I got going, the execution was easy. It was pretty much just 'wake up and walk all day.'"

After I'd been to my first fifty countries, I started writing about the quest to go everywhere, sharing my experiences on a blog. A few people began to follow along with the journey, and some wrote in to share feedback of all kinds. Most comments were positive, but I had my share of critics as well. When it comes to travel, everyone has an opinion on how to do it and the rules you should follow. One guy was dismissive: "This is easy. To go to every country, all you need is enough time and money."

He meant it as a critical comment, and at first I was upset. "Easy! This isn't easy. You try taking a thirty-hour bus ride through East Africa or a bush taxi to an overland border crossing."

But then I thought more about what lay at the core of the criticism. I once heard someone say that criticism is like a nut surrounded by a hard shell. The hard shell represents a projected experience from a biased perspective—something you should discard and ignore. If you can successfully discard the criticism's outer trappings, there is often something you can learn from its core, especially after you've allowed some time to pass.

In the case of the "time and money" comment, I realized there was a lesson I could apply. I'd always been somewhat methodical about goal setting. I spent the better part of a week every December reviewing the year that had just passed and planning ahead for the next one. The quest to visit every country came about only after I spent a lot of time thinking through the logistics. Focusing on those details—the *how* of the quest—was actually a benefit, not something to be disparaged or deemphasized. The quest was successful *because* I'd thought it through—not in spite of it.

Counting the Cost

It was true: If I broke down the overwhelming project of visiting 193 countries before the age of thirty-five into a long series of small tasks, most of the problems I had to solve became much more manageable. It all started when I first tallied the estimated cost of scaling up from 50 countries to 100 countries. I guessed that it would cost somewhere in the neighborhood of $30,000, and that it would take approximately five to seven years to complete. My first thought upon doing the math was: "Wow, that's all?"

I didn't have an extra $30,000 just lying around, but I realized that if I lived frugally, over the course of several years 100 countries wouldn't be an unobtainable goal. As I grew closer to completing that goal, I realized that it was within my grasp to actually visit *every* country. Going everywhere would be more expensive and challenging than going to a limited number of places (especially since when I set my original goal, I had the luxury of picking and choosing my destinations), but I knew it was possible by solving one problem at a time. The thought process was like this.

What if I go to every country in the world?

No way! That's impossible!

Why not? What would it take?

A lot of time . . . probably a lot of money . . . and I'll probably have to factor in certain variables I haven't considered.

How much time? How much money? What might those other variables be? Let's figure it out.

Another way to consider a big goal is to start from the end point and plan backward. The end point is your final destination—whatever you're trying to accomplish or achieve. In my case the end point would be the final country, otherwise known as number 193. What had to happen before I arrived there? Depending on which geography system you learned in school, there are either five or six permanently inhabited continents (some geographers combine Europe and Asia, and only scientists and penguins call Antarctica home). I'd need to visit each country in all of them.

In addition to finding the time and scraping together the money, I foresaw a few other big challenges. Reflecting on these hurdles led me to set subgoals. A few examples:

- Visit every country in Africa (the most challenging continent, containing more than 50 countries).
- Visit every country in Asia. (Many Asian countries are easy to get to, but not all.)
- Visit every country in the South Pacific (also a challenge, since some islands are tiny and have very limited flight schedules).
- Visit countries such as Iraq, North Korea, Somalia, and others that were in the midst of conflict or closed to most visitors. (I labeled a few of these places "rogue states and other interesting locations.")
- Visit all the "stans," including Turkmenistan, Afghanistan, and five others. (The stans are beautiful, but getting permission to visit can sometimes be difficult.)

Since it would be a ten-year journey, I couldn't stay excited on a daily basis by thinking about the finish line. That's when subgoals proved helpful. When I made it to East Timor, my final Asian country, I went on a long run and thought about all that had happened to get me there. A few years earlier, I'd never heard of East Timor. (And a few years before that, it didn't exist. Until the arrival of South Sudan in 2011, East Timor was the world's newest country.)

Getting to the "stans" had been particularly difficult. I finally arrived in Dushanbe, Tajikistan, on an Aeroflot flight from Moscow in the middle of winter. I was required to purchase a tour as part of my trip to Tajikistan, and my guides were waiting for me at the airport after a long and confusing customs interrogation. I'd arrived in the frigid capital city in February, so I dutifully bundled up and nodded appreciatively as the guides ferried me around to museums and state buildings.

When I left the country a few days later, this time returning home via Istanbul, I realized I had now completed a big and mysterious part of the world. This was it! Central Asia was now off the list.

Deductive Reasoning

You can apply the same "time and money" principle to many quests and projects. What will it take? What is required? The more specific you can be in your planning, even if you're making rough estimates, the easier it will be to get your head around the goal. What is the goal, *really*? What does success look like?

At the beginning of a quest, you should estimate the toll it will take. What will achieving your goal require?

GOAL: _____

TIME: _____

MONEY: _____

OTHER COSTS: _____

UNKNOWN: _____

While many quests are born out of spontaneity and a yearning for romance, a healthy dose of reasoning is needed if you hope to see your quest through.

❂

Matt Krause had a dream like Nate's: to walk across Turkey. Matt planned his route far in advance. "I'll be walking 60 miles a week, for a total of 22 weeks," he wrote in a detailed planning spreadsheet. The spreadsheet included data on the elevation of each day's proposed walk, as well as the climate and average temperature for all the different areas he passed through. Hard-core? Maybe. But Matt says that the granularity of the information helped him to understand what he was getting into. It also helped him demonstrate to curious people that he knew what he was doing.* It wasn't just a passing thought; it was a *plan*.

Scott Young, who taught himself the four-year MIT computer science curriculum in one year, didn't just jump into the project at first thought. "I spent nearly two months preparing the curriculum before starting my challenge," he told me, "including a one-week pilot study with a single class."

The pilot study helped with a lot of things. First, it gave Scott confidence: He could do this! It would be tough, but it wouldn't be impossible. Second, it helped him think about how to structure the rest of the commitment. He learned which times of day he was most likely to study. He considered the rest of the curriculum and visualized which parts would be more challenging. By the end of the pilot study, he felt his head was in the game and that he was ready to strike out on the full, yearlong commitment.

You can apply the time and money principle to many different projects. Let's look at a couple more examples, focusing on an idea and the expected objections to it.

---

* Read more of Matt's story in chapter 15. To see his detailed spreadsheet, visit HeathenPilgrim.com/the-route.

Quest: To walk the Camino de Santiago

Since medieval times, pilgrims have embarked on an extended hike along the Camino de Santiago in Spain, also known as the Way of St. James. Most pilgrims walk at least a few miles a day, stopping at cheap hostels each night before continuing the journey early the next morning.

Time: Approximately seven weeks.

Cost: Variable, but can be done for as little as $20 per day.

Obstacle Number One: Uncertain about walking long distances. ("Can I really walk 503 miles?")

Way Around It: Practice walking a few miles a day, and fit in one longer walk a week. Research and purchase walking shoes that provide good support.

Obstacle Number Two: Not sure how it works. ("How do I get to Spain? Do I do this on my own or with a group?")

Way Around It: Read up. Gain confidence. Talk to someone else who has done it.

Quest: To learn a new language in a short period of time

The semiprofessional language learners I talked to for this book each have different methods, but they all agree on the fundamentals: Anyone can learn new languages, and it doesn't take as long as most people expect.

Time: Six months (or whatever you decide).

Cost: Variable, but can be done very affordably and possibly even for free.

Obstacle Number One: Lack of confidence. ("I'm not good at speaking other languages.")
Way Around It: Begin slowly. Ask for help. Accept that everyone starts as a beginner.

Obstacle Number Two: Uncertain how to proceed. ("Do I take a course? Get a tutor? Download some podcasts?")
Way Around It: Attempt all of those things and see what works best for you. Just start!

Obstacle Number Three: Perception of not enough time. ("I'm too busy.")
Way Around It: Incorporate it into your regular routine. Carry a stack of index cards with new vocabulary. Listen to music in the language you want to learn. Study in ten-minute breaks whenever you can make the time.

But What About Spontaneity?

One of my favorite poems is "Ithaca." Composed in 1911 by the Greek poet Constantine Cavafy, its story is loosely based on Homer's *Odyssey,* but with principles for any traveler or sojourner. The thirty-six-line poem is full of lessons on choosing a purpose, proceeding with abandon, and ignoring critics. One of my favorite parts illuminates how to value both journey and destination:

> *Always keep Ithaca on your mind.*
> *To arrive there is your ultimate goal.*
> *But do not hurry the voyage at all.*

> *It is better to let it last for many years;*
> *and to anchor at the island when you are old,*
> *rich with all you have gained on the way,*
> *not expecting that Ithaca will offer you riches.*

If you're sailing to Ithaca, there will be plenty of time for spontaneity and surprise. The goal is your driver, that thing you propel yourself toward. It doesn't mean that you won't change course or do something fun and different along the way.

Yes, it's all about the journey and voyage, but having a destination in mind will help. Thinking logically about your goals and breaking down the obstacles is good for you. If you're going to run a race, you should plan. The more prepared you are, the more spontaneous you can be.

Annual Review

Every year since 2006, I've set aside an entire week in December to review the year that has almost ended and prepare for the next. More than anything else I do, this exercise helped to keep me on track with the round-the-world quest, as well as many other projects.

The review begins with a set of journaling exercises, focused on two questions:

What went well this year?
What did not go well this year?

A core principle of the review is that we tend to overestimate what we can accomplish in a single day, but underestimate what can happen in a year. Even if it's been a tough year, I'm always surprised as I reflect on completed projects that were hatched six or nine months earlier. It's also good to pay attention to what didn't go well, since ideally you'd like to avoid some of those things the next year.

I jot down at least ten to twelve answers for each of the two questions, focusing on successes, struggles, and projects—whether completed, in progress, or stalled. This leads to the next, longer stage of the planning process where I look ahead to the forthcoming year, thinking about which projects I'd like to pursue and which actions I need to take to ensure their success.

I then set a number of goals based on specific categories. Your own categories may vary, but some of mine include:

Writing
Business
Friends and Family
Service
Travel
Spiritual
Health
Learning
Financial (Earning)
Financial (Giving)
Financial (Saving)

The review takes place over a week, while I'm not doing as much other work. Thinking through the categories one by one, I set an average of three to five measurable goals for each. A few examples include:

- Maintain running fitness of fifteen to thirty miles per week, and run at least one half marathon
- Tour to meet readers in at least twenty-five cities
- Increase income by 20 percent or more (usually based on a specific project)
- Read at least forty books
- Publish at least one hundred blog posts

Toward the end of the week, after I've set thirty to fifty goals across my various categories, I define the overall outcomes for the year ahead. One year from now, what do I want to have accomplished?

I usually write this statement as a short paragraph. Here's an example from a few years ago:

> *Outcomes: At the end of 2009 I will have finished the manuscript for my first book and published 100 essays on the AONC [Art of Non-Conformity] blog. I will have visited 20 new countries, recovered from my running injury to complete a fourth marathon (or two half marathons), and built a new small business that supports my primary writing goals.*

I also choose a word or overall theme for the year. Past years have been dubbed "The Year of Learning" (when I finished a graduate degree), "The Year of Convergence" (as I sought to tie together a number of unrelated projects), and "The Year of Scale and Reach" (where I began touring more extensively, hosting or speaking at seventy events with readers around the world).

Of course, you can adapt the above review for your own

purposes. A good plan allows for plenty of spontaneity and room for change—but without a plan at all, it's difficult to work toward something significant over time. As several people in this book have argued, planning well and being specific with your intentions is a great help as you progress through your journey.*

Numbers Are Your Friends

A marathon is 26.2 miles or 42.2 kilometers. Before the race, you focus your training on the numbers: "This weekend I'm going to do eighteen," you might say, referring to the number of miles on your weekly long run. "During the week I'll be running three, six, four, and six."

At the end of the race, each mile matters. I didn't run my second marathon well, and by the time I reached mile 22 I didn't feel triumphant—I felt exhausted and I had a hard time finishing the final 4.2 miles. A couple of years later I ran a much slower pace in another marathon, but I felt much better at the end.

If you want to climb every mountain, you need to know how many there are. If you want to see every bird on earth (or at least as many as possible), you need to understand the taxonomy of birds.

Does it just become about ticking things off a list? Not really—or at least it shouldn't. But the list keeps you focused. A measurable goal is a good companion, and the numbers are your friends.

---

* For an expanded version of this exercise with a free template for your own annual review, visit FindtheQuest.com.

Alternative: Forget Planning, Just Start

While it's probably best to count the cost before undertaking a lifelong commitment, you can also end up mired in planning paralysis. If you're predisposed to overthink, the answer is simple: Just do it.

Tom Allen, the bike guy who left England for foreign lands, says that almost every day he hears from people who write in to ask how they can follow a similar passion. For a long time he dutifully answered their questions, which were often about gear and packing. After a while, though, he realized that this wasn't the real problem. Asking "What gear do you use?" is the wrong question, he says. The better question is "What are you waiting for?"

He created a detailed handbook that answered all the technical questions, available for purchase on his website. But he's also quick to say that the technical problems can be solved along the way. His best advice has now been simplified: "Pick a departure date. Start saving. Get a bike, tent, and sleeping bag. And go."

Gabriel Wyner, an engineering student turned professional opera singer, succeeded in learning four languages by following a true immersion process. He started with a German language camp at Middlebury College in Vermont, which hosts a number of different summer programs. Immersion means nonstop immersion: All students sign a pledge to speak *only* the new language they are learning for the entire time they are there, including evenings and weekends. No exceptions!

Total immersion is awkward and frustrating at first . . . but then it gets better. Gabriel started with "Hallo" and went from there. After a few days, the language learning affected his dream life. Every night he'd dream of the same interactions in his limited vocabulary: "Hi. My name is Gabriel. What's your name? I like pizza. Do you like pizza?" (They were pretty much the most boring dreams you could imagine, he says.)

Over time, though, the immersion process worked its magic. Gabriel now speaks five languages comfortably and is embarking on his sixth. He also offers the same lesson as Tom and many others: Jump in with both feet. Stop making excuses.

❂

After I'd visited more than sixty countries, I settled into a routine. It was a strange routine, perhaps, but there were repeating patterns and ongoing tasks. I'd prepare for a trip, often fighting a battle over visas and receiving my passport back from the agency just before departure. The time it took to pack my bag grew shorter with each trip. I learned that I could wear the same clothes most places—and if I forgot something, I could probably find what I needed along the way.

Then I'd come home and prepare to travel again. More countries down, more countries to plan for a future trip. I remembered what Nate said about walking across America: All he had to do was get up every morning and walk. In my case, all I had to do was get myself to the Central African Republic.

Meanwhile, the struggles that Nate experienced on his walk across America were pretty much what he expected: loneliness, the fear of not having a place to sleep at night, and the physical challenge of wearing a backpack and walking all day.* He kept going, though. Every day, he'd get up and walk. Something interesting would probably happen at some point during the day, but even if it didn't, he'd still get closer to the Pacific Ocean by putting one foot in front of the other. The trek took seven and a half months, but 3,200 miles after leaving his home in Maine, Nate arrived at the San Francisco Bay. The journey was over.

Remember

Ask yourself what it will cost to follow your dream. Get specific. Be sure to clearly understand the time, money, and other costs before you begin.

Generate confidence by listing the questions that your project provokes, and also the objections that you'll want to deal with in advance.

Planning is good . . . but if you spend all your time planning without making progress, try *doing* something instead.

---

* Nate is a soft-spoken, laid-back guy. When we followed up with him during fact-checking about the challenges he experienced, he mentioned he'd also been charged by a bear. "How could you leave that out earlier?" I asked. "Well, it just didn't seem like much of a challenge," he said.

Chapter 8

Life Listing

We like lists because we don't want to die.
—UMBERTO ECO

Lesson: WE'RE MOTIVATED BY PROGRESS
AND ACHIEVEMENT. IT FEELS GOOD TO
CHECK THINGS OFF.

In 2007, the film *The Bucket List* premiered, starring Jack Nicholson and Morgan Freeman. In the film, two old men with terminal diagnoses set off to fulfill a "bucket list"—the things one of the men hoped to do before dying. The film received mixed reviews but has had a pop-culture afterlife in at least one respect. The phrase "bucket list" was in use before the movie came out, but since then it's become much more common and known.

A number of websites cropped up, providing users with an opportunity to create their own list of "Things to Do Before You Die." A few years later, the "quantified self" movement attracted followers interested in documenting their lives to an extreme degree. I'm not very sophisticated in the life tracking or quantified self movements, but I've noticed that even the occasional use of it can be helpful. For example, I use an app on my phone to track my running, especially the longer runs that I do most

Sunday mornings. On a recent eight-mile run, I noticed that my pace was consistently around 8:34 per mile. At the six-mile point, I decided it would be fun to aim for an average pace of 8:30 or less. Since I only had two miles left, this would require those final miles to be run much faster than the others. Alas, I slowed down and had to walk for part of the seventh mile, thus decreasing my average overall pace to 8:36. For the final mile, I faced an even greater challenge: To achieve the 8:30 goal, I'd need to run *much* faster than I had for the past hour.

I ended up meeting the goal and finishing with an average pace of 8:29. Due to the final-mile sprint, I was more tired than usual at the end, but I also experienced a sense of satisfaction. The point? Without the ability to track my pace and record it for all posterity (that is, posting it for the two friends who followed my running times through the same app), I wouldn't have had the goal of pushing myself at the end and thus getting a better workout.

Your basic *life list*—a term we'll use as a synonym for bucket list—isn't a bad start. But what if you could go further? What if you organized your life around a single, principal focus or aim?

You know how you meet people and they ask, "What do you do?" You can always say that you're a teacher or a student, an accountant or an artist, or whatever your vocation. But once you have a quest, you have another answer, too. Your identity isn't tied to a job; your identity is who you really are.

I'm trying to visit every country in the world.
I'm on a quest to publish one million processed photos.
I'm going to produce the largest symphony ever performed.

The Personal Annual Reports
of
Nicholas Felton

Every year since 2004, a New York City designer named Nicholas Felton has chronicled his life in a series of personal annual reports. The reports are extremely extensive and include a number of statistics on his activities over the past year. Felton captures the data through a series of check-ins he uploads from his phone at random intervals every day. The number of data points is amazing: He captures everything he eats and drinks, his precise location at all times, daily sleep hours, and countless other facts.

This project is more about recording than influencing behavior. As Nicholas explained, when he started compiling the information each year, he felt inspired to "say yes" to activities he might normally decline. The reports are highly regimented in their display of data, but Nicholas doesn't believe this causes him to do the same thing all the time. In fact, it's the opposite: "I think the reports have made me much more aware of my routines and grateful when I can break from them," he said.

Learn more at Feltron.com.

Regardless of how it begins, a quest provides a focal point. Once you have a task to pursue, you have a new way of looking at the world, a new point of identity. Phoebe Snetsinger, the record-setting birder, traveled to dozens of countries. But

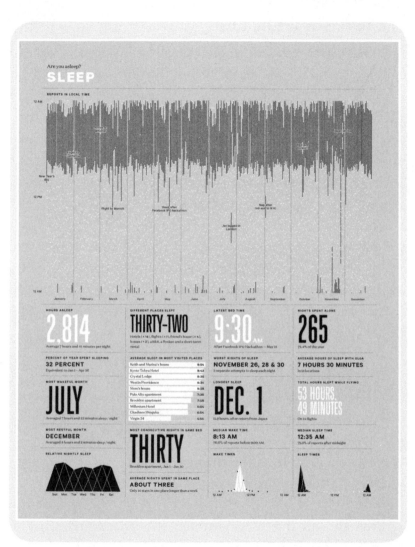

she went to the ends of the earth not for the sake of traipsing through war zones and jungles; she went where the birds
were. As she put it, the quest gave her "a purpose in my me-
anderings."

The Twenty-Year Life List

In 1994, sixteen-year-old Kristen Goldberg made her first and only life list. This was years before *The Bucket List* had hit theaters, and Kristen didn't know anyone else who was making a list. It just seemed like a fun project.

Twenty years later, Kristen is still following the same list—no modifications permitted, even though some items might not be as important to a thirty-six-year-old woman as they were to a sixteen-year-old teenager.

The original list included twenty-three life experiences, and every year she picks two or three to work on. Some were clearly written by a teenager ("Visit a nude beach" appears on the list, an item to which Kristen now says "Thanks a lot, sixteen-year-old self") but others have remained lifelong aspirations. Items on her list include:

- Learn Japanese
- Take a course in self-defense
- Visit Salzburg
- Win big in Las Vegas
- Go to a drive-in movie theater
- Plant a tree on my wedding day

Even though the list didn't tell Kristen exactly what to do or how to live, it has had considerable impact on her life. As part of the original project, Kristen hoped to visit all fifty states. When I talked with her she'd been to thirty-three. Her husband picked the spot where he proposed based on how it would help her cross an item off the list.

Even as she works as a teacher, Kristen relies on the list

as a guidepost. Every year she teaches a freshman seminar for her fifteen-year-old students. At the end of the class she shows the *Bucket List* film, shares her story about the list she made as a teenager, and invites students to create lists of their own. Item by item, year after year, she continues to complete the original list from two decades ago.

The Yearlong Quest

A. J. Jacobs popularized an entire genre of modern-day short-term-quest literature. After his book on reading the *Encyclopedia Britannica, The Know-It-All,* became a bestseller, he found a pattern he could replicate for other projects. Another book, *The Year of Living Biblically,* was also a huge hit.

Since A.J.'s popularization of the short-term quest, a countless number of followers have trod the same path, and many have chronicled their explorations in books or movies. A very partial list includes:

- *Julie and Julia: My Year of Cooking Dangerously.* Julie Powell sets out to make 524 recipes in a year—every recipe from Julia Child's classic French cookbook.
- *A Simple Act of Gratitude: How Learning to Say Thank You Changed My Life.* Lawyer John Kralik is on the down-and-out, struggling with divorce and a failing career. Over the next year he practices gratitude by writing 365 detailed thank-you notes to people he encounters.
- *Dream On: One Hack Golfer's Challenge to Break Par in a Year.* John Richardson has a full-time job and a family, but does everything he can to improve his golf

game over the course of a year. Will he make it? Spoiler: He does. But as with any good memoir, the joy is in the struggle and the lessons.

- *Not Buying It: My Year Without Shopping.* Judith Levine and her partner, Paul, spend a year without purchasing anything except that which is completely necessary for living. Along the way they learn various lessons and question society.
- *Living Oprah: My One-Year Experiment to Walk the Walk of the Queen of Talk.* Robyn Okrant, a "thirty-five-year-old average American woman," devotes a year to following all of Oprah Winfrey's advice. What happens when the advice conflicts? You'll just have to read the book.

Are these kinds of pursuits really quests? Perhaps it depends on your motivation. If you pursue the project primarily for your personal development or curiosity, it's a quest. If your primary goal is to write a book, produce a documentary, or otherwise publicize your quest, maybe it's more of a career move. There's nothing wrong with doing something for your career—but it's not really a *quest,* since a quest requires sacrifice and uncertainty.

Fifty Dates in Fifty States

Alicia Ostarello had recently seen a promising relationship come to an unexpected end, and was once again looking for love. Frustrated with online dating in San Francisco, where everyone she met seemed similar, she thought about exploring her horizons. At the same time, she was unhappy with her job writing copy twelve hours a day for a startup. The time for change was ripe, and she hoped to combine travel with an experiment in relationships.

Alicia would hit the road and visit all fifty states, having one date per state and journaling about the experience. She would see the country and meet new people. "Not to generalize too much," she said, "But I was fairly certain that farmers in North Dakota would be different from tech guys in the Bay Area."

It was the perfect short-term quest, with a clear goal and end point and the chance for plenty of self-discovery and spontaneity along the way. The project turned into a documentary, with a young filmmaker traveling along with her.

Initial progress took longer than expected. "I was ready to hit the road right away," Alicia told me, "but getting things in order for the documentary and travel plans required that we reset our initial calendar." They finally agreed to travel throughout the lower forty-eight states in a Honda Fit, then fly to Alaska and Hawaii to complete the journey.

Surveying the romantic possibilities of fifty states wasn't a lifelong quest, but it was meaningful and interesting. On the road Alicia and her filmmaker companion dutifully met guys from Alabama to Wyoming and every state in between. Every day one of them would post a blog entry about the events of the day and what they had observed.

Level Up Your Life

Steve Kamb is a real-life Clark Kent turned Superman. Growing up in Atlanta, he earned a degree in economics and was headed for what he described as "a normal, boring life." Nothing was wrong with that life, he says now, but it just wasn't interesting.

Until a couple of years ago, Steve had never been outside of North America. He ate the same food every day and was uncomfortable in social situations. Emerging from a phone booth one day—or at least rolling out of bed at the crack of nine a.m.—Steve set out to make a series of real changes. Having grown up glued to the TV and computer screen, he modeled his quest on a video game. Here's how Steve explains it:

I'm on an Epic Quest of Awesome to level up my life in all aspects: travel, personal health, wealth, language learning, and more. The entire quest is structured like a giant video game in which I'm the character. I earn "experience points" every time I cross an item off my list, whenever I complete five items I "level up" (I'm currently up to Level 10!), each continent is a different "level," and there are "master quests" that are more difficult than the others.

The first items on Steve's list were easy. He had to get off the couch and get in shape, beginning a new lifestyle of living actively and looking past the potato chips at the grocery store. As he gained confidence and experience points, the tasks become harder—but also more fun.

One of the tasks was "Complete a James Bond weekend." To accomplish it, Steve used hotel points to check into a luxury casino resort in Monte Carlo. He changed out of his usual outfit of T-shirt and flip-flops, rented a tuxedo that required the purchase of fancy dress shoes, and strolled into the casino. Not used to the life of the ultrarich in the French Riviera, he wasn't sure what to do next—but he knew that projecting confidence was an important part of being James Bond. He walked over to the blackjack table, slapped down $200, and said "Deal me in."*

The structure of Steve's "game" made it fun and rewarding. "By assigning point values and structuring the whole list like a game," he told me, "it tapped into that part of my brain that loved to level up in video games. But instead of playing a game, it got me addicted to crossing more things off the list and always working toward the next quest."

Steve's quest has inspired a legion of followers, who post their own goals and progress on the forums of NerdFitness .com, a website he started after pursuing the quest on his own. As his exploits became popular, Steve began to receive offers for support from all over the world. The offers were great, but they also presented a dilemma: His goal wasn't to freeload. He'd started the quest as a DIY project, and it was important to prove that he could do it on his own. If he had sponsors, he suspected it wouldn't feel as personal.

One day he realized that there were important distinctions among the offers that were coming in. He didn't want to be funded by Nike or travel the world with an obligation to write favorable articles about companies that were paying his way. At the same time, offers to stay with readers seemed more meaningful.

Once he thought about it in those terms, it was easy to split the difference. When a reader offered him a couch in Singapore, he gladly accepted. When a tourism department offered a ten-day, all-expenses-paid trip to Jordan, he politely declined.

The quest has continued to the point where Steve strives

---

*At the end of the weekend, Steve donated the shoes to a panhandler and changed back into his flip-flops.

to achieve higher and higher goals. He learned Portuguese and attended the carnival festival in Brazil. He piloted a stunt plane and went on an African safari. At the top of the list: "Purchase a small island." It's a big goal, but Steve's level-up structure keeps him motivated and on track.

Your First (or Tenth) Life List

What if we could come to the end of our lives and, looking back on our rich history of experiences, relationships, and accomplishments, feel truly fulfilled? Either metaphorically or literally, what if we could point to a list of steadily pursued dreams that had turned into accomplished goals?

One of the ways we can ensure this happens is to clearly identify the activities that help us feel alive. Writing a *life list* can help us to live. If you've never made such a list before, there's no time like the present, and there's no single way to do it. A life list is simply a list of long-term personal goals, often expressed as "Things to do before I die." You simply devote an hour, or however long it takes, to thinking about your life. How do you want to spend it? What do you want to experience along the way? Then you make a list of anything that comes to mind, without self-editing as you go. It's your list, so do it in your own way—but here are a few tips that may help.

> **Avoid fuzzy goals.** Make your list specific! Many goals are basic and unmeasurable: to lose weight, save money, or have better posture are all good things, but they're also somewhat fuzzy and vague. Far better are goals like "Meet the Dalai Lama" or "See the northern lights." If

you set specific goals, you'll know exactly when you've accomplished them.

Mix it up. Don't just make a note about climbing Everest because other people have done it—think about what you *really* want to do. Some adventure goals are good, but be sure you have other goals as well. In trying to figure out what to put on your life list, think, "What do I really want to be, do, and achieve?" Remember, the idea is to dream big and avoid limitations. You can be in the Formula 1 *and* write a novel. The fewer limits you place on your list, the better it will be.

~~Be realistic.~~ **Think big.** The life list is for your whole life! As you compose your list, remember that the basic rule of brainstorming is "Don't limit yourself." You should also avoid thinking about your present situation. This is your whole life list; it's meant to be something you work on and refer to for a long time. In other words, discard reality . . . or more precisely, what you think of as reality. As your journey progresses, you may very well find that what you thought was reality was actually quite limiting.

As much as possible, you should also ignore fear when you write your life list. Fear of failure, and even the fear of success, holds us back from attempting many of the things we secretly wish for. If what you have in mind seems daunting, just tell yourself "It's only a list."

Building a Structure

I asked readers to share some of the items on their lists. Many fit into a few obvious categories:

Travel or Adventure

- See the northern lights
- Overcome a fear of heights and go skydiving
- Visit every UNESCO World Heritage site
- Antarctica!
- Ride in a helicopter

Active

- Climb Mount Rainier
- Complete yoga teacher training
- Swim with a whale shark
- Learn to surf

Personal Development

- Get out of debt
- Go to the opera
- Become a barista
- Sponsor a child
- Get a tattoo

Academic/Creative

- Graduate from college, university, or graduate school
- Publish a short story
- Learn to speak French (or Chinese, or any other foreign language)

Finally, a few unexpected responses seem worth noting:

- Attempt flight using a deck chair and balloons
- Hijack a parade and lead a special dance

- Drive a Zamboni
- Win a watermelon seed–spitting contest
- Hug a panda
- Play the ukulele on stage at the White House
- Ride an ostrich while racing a kangaroo at 40+ mph
  (Bonus points: Win the race.)

Your list belongs to you, so feel free to make it up entirely on your own. But if you're looking for inspiration, you can find more than three hundred other responses at FindtheQuest.com.

❂

Every good goal has a deadline, so let's put a deadline on some of these ideas.

Goal:
Deadline:
Next Step:

All you need is one next step. Don't worry about thinking the whole thing through yet.

❂

When Steve began his "Epic Quest of Awesome," the pursuit did more than help him get in shape. Kristen's "life list from her sixteen-year-old self" has survived more than sixteen years later. Can a simple list give you purpose and grounding? Don't knock it until you try it. If nothing else, it's a great starting point to becoming more intentional with your life.

Remember

———

A quest can provide a focal point or purpose.

We feel motivated by making lists and checking things off.

A good life list should include goals in multiple categories, not just travel or adventure.

Chapter 9

Forward Motion

Damn, that was a long-ass journey!
—Homer's ODYSSEY, Standard Portland English

Lesson: "QUESTS ARE BORING.
ALL YOU HAVE TO DO IS PUT ONE FOOT
IN FRONT OF THE OTHER."

In a series of stories that were eventually recorded as *The Odyssey*, Greek poet Homer chronicled dozens of adventures, both big and small. These adventures took place over more than ten years and have achieved an immortality in Western culture. While the entire journey is recorded in a nonlinear form, a rough chronology is as follows:

Year 1: After a long battle, Odysseus and his men leave Troy and attempt to return home, immediately encountering various problems.

Years 2–8: Odysseus is captured and held prisoner on the island of Ogygia for seven long years. Bummer. He eventually engineers his escape from the island in true reality-show fashion.

Years 9–10: But then! More bad stuff happens. An increasingly poor set of decisions prolongs the journey and delays the homecoming. Odysseus falls in love with the wrong girl. Odysseus seeks navigation advice from a blind poet—because a blind man is obviously the best person to ask when you're lost. Odysseus learns as he goes. The hero channels his inner powers and obtains occasional help from the gods. ("Use the force, Odysseus.") After escaping various perilous situations, he finds his way back to the road home.

Sometime Later (Chronology Uncertain): Odysseus returns home! In a classic big-summer-movie finale, he kills the suitors who've been pestering his long-ignored wife Penelope, reunites with her, and says hello to the family dog. Relatives of the dead suitors raise a minor ruckus, but the goddess Athena shows up and tells everyone to stand down. Order is restored.*

It's a great story (and the extended version is even better), but consider everything that is quickly glossed over: countless months sailing the sea with no monsters to fight or forbidden fruit to ignore . . . seven long years in prison . . . endless back and forth. No matter how you look at it, in Odysseus's journey there was a lot of waiting around for things to happen.

"Give me a place to stand and I will move the earth," wrote Homer in *The Iliad,* the prequel to his surprise bestseller *The Odyssey.* But what he left out was all that time sailing in the wrong direction or waiting around in prison for the gods to finally show up and lend a hand.

---

* English teachers, please direct complaints regarding the condensed *Odyssey* timeline to Random House, 1745 Broadway, New York, NY 10019.

In modern-day quests and adventures, Athena doesn't usually make any cameos, but like with Homer's journey there *is* a lot of monotonous detail that often doesn't garner attention. Take running a marathon, for example. The course is 26.2 miles or 42.2 kilometers, but many runners—or at least one author, who has occasionally attempted marathons—believe that the race doesn't really begin until mile 18. Up to that point, you're just cruising along, putting down mile after mile, and the time passes somewhat uneventfully.

Ultrarunners speak of the transformation that takes hold of their bodies after completing even longer distances. If they're lucky, at a certain point they enter a trancelike state, jacked up on the natural high of endorphins as they run mile after mile. But as they look back at all those long training runs, ranging farther and farther from home weekend after weekend, many also talk of the monotony that comes with the task.

Remember Nate Damm's experience of walking across America, day in and day out for months: "Execution was easy," he told me. "Once I got going, it was pretty much just 'wake up and walk all day.'"

What Nate came to learn is what Odysseus learned, or what anyone who has ever climbed a mountain has learned: The path to the summit consists of repetitive movements, but it is precisely the arduousness of the task that makes the accomplishment an epic one.

Forward, Onward

Experience produces confidence, and confidence produces success. I didn't decide to visit every country until I'd been to more than fifty. After I traveled for a while, I was able to cope with whatever challenge my itinerary presented. I was shaken down for bribes in Guinea and Sierra Leone, but successfully resisted most of the arm twisting. I learned the art of sleeping on the floor of airports in Rome and Romania.

In some ways, visiting every country became more difficult as I worked my way down to the last countries on my list. I'd run out of easy stops. Almost everywhere I needed to go required an advance visa, a complicated flight itinerary, or both. Whereas I'd started the quest by regularly visiting as many as five countries in a single two-week trip, by the end I was flying all over the world just to get to a single new country.

In other ways, though, the quest became *easier* as I went along. The variables decreased since I needed to visit fewer places. If you want to visit all of Africa, you've got a huge riddle to solve. There are fifty-four independent countries on the continent, many originally divided on political lines instead of geographical ones, creating a wealth of problems. Several countries are in ongoing disputes with their neighbors, so instead of going logically from one country to another, you often have to fly to a third country to transit.

In short, it's a mess. But once you get down to a few remaining countries, your options are very clear. There aren't many ways to get to Gambia. You can fly to Dakar, Senegal, and then hop over on a ferry or commuter flight, or you can take the twice-weekly flight from London. That's it.

My love of travel hacking helped me memorize airline schedules to the point where I became an annoying party guest, asking people who were going on a trip for their full itinerary and offering unsolicited advice.

As I gained confidence, I stopped worrying about things. I rerouted trips from the middle of Madagascar. When embassies turned down my visa applications, I flew to countries anyway in hopes of making it work on the ground. (Most of the time, it did.) I was fully invested in completing the quest, and I found I was making progress more quickly than expected.

Faster, Stronger

Others in this book experienced the same phenomenon of rapid advancement. Phoebe Snetsinger, who set out to see as many bird species as possible, initially planned to take two or three foreign trips a year, seeing a few hundred birds annually. This quickly expanded once she had a few foreign trips under her belt and was hooked. "Numbers were piling up," she wrote. "My biggest total year had been the previous one, when I'd seen nearly 1,000 new species, about the maximum I could possibly absorb and hope to retain."

Robyn Devine, who is undertaking a long project to make 10,000 hand-knit hats, began with a much smaller project to knit 100 hats in a year. But just as I learned what I was truly capable of once I'd traveled to fifty countries, she discovered she could make many more. "I thought 100 hats would be a huge challenge," she wrote, "But it was surprisingly easy. That's when I knew I needed a *real* challenge." The logical step from 100 would be 1,000, but that still seemed too easy. "A thousand was doable," she continued, "But when I thought about 10,000, I realized it would be a massive goal. That's why I wanted to do it!"*

Having a way to measure your goal is critical. Whenever I went to a new country, I'd pull up an Evernote file listing the *Wikipedia* count of all 193 countries. I put a bold X next to each completed country, as well as the total number of completed countries at the top. As the list moved from $150/193$ to $175/193$ . . . and then inched closer to the final ten countries, I felt a surge of accomplishment.†

In some ways, the quest was monotonous, but that was the point! I liked the monotony. I liked the routine. I also learned a key skill of travel. More important than the ability to speak a lot of languages (not my forte) or competence in packing everything in a small carry-on bag (it gets easy when you pack and unpack every day) is the ability to wait. Once you make your peace with waiting—sometimes for hours on end with no clear resolution in sight—the traveling life becomes much easier.

Three Hundred Marathons and Counting (But Why?)

John "Maddog" Wallace qualifies as an obsessive. For the past three decades he has been running . . . and running . . . and running. A former smoker, John could hardly run at all when he began. When he ran his first marathon in Reno, Nevada, he hit the infamous "long-distance wall" and struggled through the final 4.2 miles. At the finish, he said to anyone who'd

---

*You can sign up to request one of your own hats at SheMakesHats.com. It will take approximately twenty-eight years to make all ten thousand, so be prepared to wait.

†People sometimes ask what I'll do when new countries crop up. Fortunately, this doesn't happen very often. In the past ten years, only two new countries have been recognized (East Timor and South Sudan).

listen, "I'm never doing that again!" (First lesson: Don't make resolutions immediately after finishing your first big race.)

When I first started reading about Mr. Maddog, I thought the next part of the story would be something like this: "A few months after the first marathon experience, he started running again, this time learning to run smarter. Gradually, he grew to appreciate the idea of running another long race. Eventually he was hooked."

But people like Maddog are not like you or me. Most of the story I had in mind turned out to be true, with one small exception. Instead of waiting a few months to ease into running again, Maddog waited *two days*. Then, instead of registering for another race several months away, he signed up for the Sacramento marathon . . . merely two weeks later. Most doctors and running coaches would advise against such a feat, but Maddog finished the race nine minutes faster than the first.*

For his third marathon, Maddog had the good sense to wait longer—this time a whole three weeks. He ran the San Francisco marathon, observing the harbor from the Golden Gate Bridge as he strode through the last miles.

The next year he moved to Dallas and joined a running group where he was first given the nickname "Maddog" because of his persistence and hyper-accelerated racing schedule. Maddog ran more marathons, holding up better and gaining confidence. Over time, the goal just took hold: He would run *everywhere*.

At age fifty-four he officially began a quest. He has now run more than three hundred marathons in more than one

_____
* Obligatory disclaimer: Unless you're an experienced runner, and also insane, do not attempt to replicate Maddog's race schedule.

hundred countries. For good measure, he also ran a marathon in all fifty U.S. states—twice!

Another committed athlete, Martin Parnell, worked his way up to an even bigger goal. He started by cycling from Cairo to Cape Town, stopping along the way to experience a way of life much different from the small town he called home in Alberta, Canada. The high point was playing table tennis with a twelve-year-old boy in an African village. "Over one hundred kids yelled and cheered as we played the game," Martin told me. "At that point I realized the power of sport and play."

Martin lost the Ping-Pong match but completed his cycling trip in Cape Town, excited about the possibilities of undertaking more big trips in the name of charity. He was drawn to the idea of quests and designed an entire series of them, partially constructed around the criteria established by Guinness World Records.

Martin's goal is to raise at least $1 million for a children's charity he supports. His 2013 goals included climbing Mount Kilimanjaro in twenty-four hours instead of the usual five days (by the way, this will be *after* running the Kilimanjaro marathon), and competing in seven trail-running or mountain-biking events.

While I was checking out his blog, where he posts updates several times each week, I noticed that he was facing a tough decision: to sign up for an upcoming fifty-kilometer race in Calgary, or to set the Guinness World Record for running the fastest marathon time in a lacrosse uniform.

In 2010 he ran 250 marathons in a single year—perhaps his most impressive feat of all.

Hey, slow down! I wanted to say to Martin. Or don't slow

down, since it seems that people like Martin never slow down. But as I had with Maddog, I wondered why was he doing all of these things. Why not raise money another way, or otherwise stay active without killing yourself all the time?

Unfortunately, emailing with Maddog and Martin didn't yield the precise answers I wanted. Like many obsessives, they both seemed to recognize that their projects are unusual, but their exact motivations are hard to pin down. It reminded me of when I was first traveling. I just wanted to do it! It was an internal drive that I couldn't ignore. The scope of the task felt challenging and exciting.

I finally asked Martin to tell me something that he found especially difficult, and here's what he said.

> *The toughest time was in the summer of 2010. It was July and the rains came and never stopped. The rain pounding on my bedroom window would wake me up and I knew that once I started running I'd be soaked within ten minutes and stay that way for another five hours. I was stiff and sore from the previous four marathons that week and all I wanted to do was stay in bed with a cup of tea and the newspaper.*

What do you think he did next? If you guessed that he went out in the rain and ran his fifth marathon of the week, you'd be right.

The One-Year MIT Challenge

I met Scott Young on a freezing night in Winnipeg, Manitoba, the coldest capital city of North America. It was January and

Shoes by the Door = Instant Accountability

On the road, I'm frequently tired from long flights, time zone changes, and the occasional tequila drink. Upon entering my hotel or guesthouse room, the first thing I do is unpack—no relaxing or checking email just yet! Whatever I expect to need for the rest of my stay gets placed in one or two areas, usually a workstation at the desk and one side of the closet for clothes. Then, if I know I should exercise, I remove my running shoes and place them by the door. This accomplishes two goals at once: First, it's one less thing I have to worry about when waking up tired to hit the gym or nearby sand dunes. Second, it creates instant accountability. I *could* skip the exercise, but I'll have to look at my shoes every time I head out the door, and I'll have to repack them later.

Putting the shoes by the door is a good way to make sure you don't take the easy way out. Maddog Wallace chose an even more effective way to make himself accountable: He told everyone what he was doing, and they watched. Even better—or worse, on the hard days—they counted on him to finish the task.

the hotel staff warned me not to leave my face uncovered for long if I went outside. Scott was a native, though: When we went to a restaurant, I remained bundled up in coat, scarf, and gloves while he dressed in a T-shirt.

Scott was a recent college graduate who had long been drawn to independent learning. He'd studied abroad in France, and was in the process of documenting some of his "learn anything quickly" methods for anyone who was interested.

His big experiment went much further than a year abroad.

Scott had begun work on a business, but was interested in computer science as well. It's hard to change your major to a challenging subject in the late phase of your undergraduate education (most people do it the other way, switching to an easier subject when a tough one proves too hard), so when Scott finished his degree he felt like he was missing something.

Going back for another four-year degree was an unattractive and expensive option. Since he enjoyed independent learning, Scott looked around for alternatives. That's when he found his quest: He'd master the world-renowned MIT computer science curriculum on his own. Every lecture and test was online for public viewing, but almost no one completed the program in its entirety. Instead, they'd typically take a look at the exams, complete a few sample questions, or perhaps complete a single course out of curiosity.*

Scott's aim was higher. With no exceptions or exemptions, he would take on the entire curriculum and fulfill all the school's requirements. It wasn't the same experience as actually *going* to MIT—he'd lack the access to professors, computer labs, and interaction with other students—but he'd cover the same material, and the course grading was completely objective: On the computer science exams, you either got the answers right or you didn't. Finally, every good goal has a deadline, so Scott decided on one year.

---

* Why does MIT put so much course work online for free? First, because it has far more demand than supply (there is no shortage of MIT applicants). Second, it's great marketing for its other programs. Putting the course work online encourages people like Scott to take on a great challenge, and it also motivates authors of lesser stature to write about it.

Scott moved to Vancouver, a much warmer and more cosmopolitan city. Five days a week, he got up at six a.m. and immediately started studying, finishing around six p.m. with only minimal breaks. The sixth day was spent working on his business, and the seventh day was for rest.

Scott's business work was fairly public, and since he was suddenly available only once a week, he decided to post updates on the project, along with the complete exam results, to anyone who cared to see.* This decision produced mixed results. While he attracted some supporters, he also attracted a number of critics who harassed him with every post. Even though Scott posted all his work online, including the mistakes, he still heard from people who believed he was arrogant for taking on the challenge. Others disagreed with some detail of his methodology, or posted anonymous comments attacking him for no good reason.

Dealing with the criticism was a distraction and harder than doing the work itself. Nevertheless, Scott persevered. One year later, the quest was complete: He'd passed every single course, all with decent grades and several with flying colors. The critics disappeared—especially the ones who said he could never succeed. Scott looked back at all the work, all those early mornings, the exams he'd gradually become comfortable facing down. He'd done it! And then he was tired, so he went to Paris for a month's vacation.

❂

---

* See all of Scott's notes and exams at www.ScottHYoung.com/blog/mit -challenge.

As Homer tells the story, Odysseus mastered countless challenges during his twenty-year saga—challenges that included near seduction by Sirens, almost becoming a tasty snack for the Cyclops, and a tough battle when he finally made it home. He also endured a lot of monotony, with the same thing happening day in, day out. Always, though, he kept going. He kept moving forward.

One time I took the train to an airport hotel before an early morning flight the next day. My plan was to get some sleep before hopping the shuttle to the concourse at five a.m. However, I was so used to going to the airport that I forgot to get off at the hotel stop. Instead, I rode all the way to the terminal before realizing my error. *Oops.*

It wasn't a big mistake—I'd only gone about fifteen minutes out of my way. But when I got back on the train to return, I realized I had a choice: Take a stop that was farther away from my hotel, and walk the half mile in the cold, or wait on the train an extra ten minutes for the more logical stop.

I knew right away which choice I'd make: I'd choose to walk. *Better to be in control of your circumstances,* I thought. *Better to make the active choice.*

The mantra of the traveler is to make peace with waiting. The mantra of the quester is to keep moving forward. Whatever it takes, whether facing an immense challenge or spirit-sapping tedium, just keep making progress.

You, too, should proceed on your quest, choosing forward motion wherever possible. Along the way, you'll gain a few skills. You'll learn that not everything will proceed as planned, and you'll learn that everything will probably be fine when it doesn't. You'll make your peace with routine and monotony.

Remember

———

The long, hard slog is a key part of most quests.

We can't opt out of monotony, but we can choose which form it takes.

When you have the option between backtracking and making progress, choose progress.

Chapter 10

The Love of the Craft

I want to be remembered as a person who wasn't afraid to start things. —TINA ROTH EISENBERG

Lesson: EFFORT CAN BE ITS OWN REWARD.

Some people are motivated by achievement, others by process—but still others are motivated by a specific blend of both. These people are all about making things and sharing them with the world, over and over.

Why create? Because you can. Or for some people, because it's what they love to do more than anything else. They like the act of creation and the act of distribution. When they finish a task, they ask, "What's next?"

In some cases, they'll even work for free.

❂

Smart companies understand that financial compensation isn't the only reason people come to work. In an ideal world, employees show up because they enjoy working on something meaningful. The chance to build something or be part of a team working on an ambitious project can be a powerful motivator.

In the case of Ron Avitzur, a software engineer who worked

on a contract for Apple, the desire to create a project went far beyond the usual employee loyalty. Before the contract was prematurely canceled, Ron had been building a graphing calculator program in the early 1990s. He'd worked on it for a long time, investing many hours and a lot of energy. When his contract was terminated, he ceased being an employee . . . yet he wasn't ready to move on.

After he was let go, Ron discovered that his badge hadn't been deactivated and that he could still come and go in the building, which was supposed to be secure. That's when he made a decision to "uncancel" his project and keep working on it himself.

Ron recruited a colleague, Greg Robbins, whose contract had also been recently canceled. In a stroke of genius, Greg told his former manager that he was now reporting to Ron, and Ron told anyone who asked that he was now reporting to Greg.* The tag team duo of Ron and Greg worked up to sixteen hours a day on the secret project, and aside from the fib about who was reporting to whom, they never lied to anyone. When people asked what they were working on, they told the truth—garnering instant respect from other engineers and software testers, who appreciated the value of working on a project for the love of it.

As the months went by, the effort grew more intense. A deadline was coming up by which the software had to be finalized so that it could be shipped with new computers. It was one thing to make a working version of the product, but it was quite another to create a "mostly finished" version that could go out

---

* Ron: "Since that left no managers in the loop, we had no meetings and could be extremely productive."

to consumers. User testing was a challenge, since the project didn't officially exist. Then there was the small matter of getting the software loaded onto the operating system that would be installed on the computers. Finally, word was spreading about the secret project, and not everyone was happy. Another group moved into the vacant offices that Ron and Greg had been operating from, and the facilities manager grew suspicious. The researchers' badges were eventually canceled, and after a few weeks during which the two men hung around outside and waited for someone else to open the door so they could sneak in, they were warned that security would have them evicted—presumably on a more lasting basis this time.

Ron, Greg, and the growing team of conspirators met each of these challenges head-on. Other engineers would materialize to help with needed quality-assurance testing. The guy who was responsible for the final operating-system software showed up at Ron's new office at two a.m. one night with instructions on how the graphing calculator program could be included. Greg was eventually able to surreptitiously register the project as the creation of an outside vendor, getting them new badges that opened the doors.

After six months of sneaking into the building every day, eluding security, and recruiting allies, Ron and Greg saw their software ship on every new Macintosh computer, more than twenty million machines. The graphing calculator received glowing feedback from users and was even referenced by Apple executives during demonstrations. The stealth project was a complete and total victory. Ron concludes his story with the wry observation: "We wanted to make a Windows version, too, but Microsoft had better building security."

Follow the Flow

What compels someone to go into work day after day—after their contract ends, without any salary, and without an actual job? It's simple: When you find something you love to do, you don't want to let it go.

In Ron's case, it didn't matter that the project had been canceled. The project wasn't complete! He had to keep going by any means necessary. He had no mortgage to pay or kids to support, and was working so many hours that he wasn't spending much money otherwise. Providing free programming services wasn't a sustainable endeavor for the rest of his life, but for a few months he was willing to go all-in on the project he loved.

Have you ever worked on something that felt so engaging that you simply didn't want it to end? The time goes by and you don't notice. You go to bed thinking about the project, and it's the first thing on your mind when you wake up. Perhaps you wouldn't sneak into your office to work after being terminated, but if you found something you loved, you'd want to hang on to it for as long as you could.

Will this feeling last forever? Probably not. That's why you should ride the wave while you can.

Even better, what if you could create your own wave, independent of the whim of a big company or someone else's decision-making power? That's what many creative people have done. Let's meet a few.

Exhibit A: Poke the Box, 365 Days a Year

Seth Godin gets up early, makes a cup of herbal tea, and sits at a big desk overlooking the Hudson River in New York. Then he settles into work, and he doesn't get up for a long time.

Seth has hundreds of thousands of fans and at least a few notable critics, but there's one thing about him that everyone agrees on: The man is prolific. According to him, he reads, researches, and writes an average of fifteen hours a day. He publishes a post on his blog every single day, no exceptions.*

At least once a year, he publishes a book—sometimes twice or three times a year, and sometimes more than one at a time. One day, a huge box showed up at my door. It contained what Seth called his "behemoth," a seven-hundred-page, 275,000-word monster compilation of several years of his posts. In addition to the writing projects, Seth regularly launches new commercial ventures, and frequently invites students to apply for internships in which they can work on Godin projects while developing their own entrepreneurial skills. Somewhere in the process, he sleeps at least a few hours every night.

It's important to note that not all of Seth's projects are big successes. In fact, by his account he's had far more failures. He invented the first-ever videotaped aquarium and fireplace. For some reason, it wasn't a huge seller. In the early days of the Internet, he published a book entitled "Email Addresses of the Rich and Famous," which resulted in a celebrity backlash.

The lesson, as he explains it: "If I fail more than you do, I win. Built into this notion is the ability to keep playing. If you get to keep playing, sooner or later you're gonna make it succeed. The people who lose are the ones who don't fail at all, or the ones who fail so big they don't get to play again."

Seth frequently writes about the concept of *shipping*, a

---

* If anything, posting "only once a day" is restrictive for Seth. "I have about six blogable ideas a day," he says, "but people get antsy when there are a lot of unread posts in their queue."

term he uses as the means of disseminating work to the world. In Seth's worldview, art doesn't exist until it is widely shared. "I've viewed my life for twenty-five years as one more opportunity to poke the box," he says, "One more opportunity to try something different."

Exhibit B: Make the Box, a Dozen Times a Day

In the trendy Dumbo neighborhood in Brooklyn, I followed a set of emailed directions to an industrial-looking building. After riding up its creaky elevator, I entered a brightly lit coworking space with a couple of dozen people scurrying about. "Hi, Chris!" said a familiar voice. The voice belonged to Tina Roth Eisenberg, also known as Swiss Miss to her legion of fans and followers.

I'd first met Tina at a workshop I facilitated a few months earlier, and she invited me to visit her headquarters at Studiomates, the coworking space she founded in Brooklyn. As I chatted with her, I also met several other people who shared the space. Some were colleagues, working directly on projects created by Tina. Others were working entirely on their own, and just rented a workspace. Still others appeared to be in ambiguous roles, doing some of their own work and some work on Tina's projects.

At least five times a day, almost every day of the week, Tina posted a short entry on her website. Many of the entries related to new design finds from around the world that had arrived in her inbox from the fans. Tina was known as a digital curator, a person of influence who helps ideas spread with her endorsement and links.

Meanwhile, crates of temporary tattoos crowded the room,

and throughout the day various colleagues stuffed orders in envelopes.

One Friday each month, Tina hosts a popular gathering called Creative Mornings. Featuring a talk by an artist or other interesting person, the gatherings are always well attended. After starting up in New York, the talks spread to a Zurich chapter, and then to Los Angeles. Eventually there were more than fifty additional chapters worldwide, with hundreds of speakers and tens of thousands of attendees taking part. It's essentially a global salon of ideas and community, with event costs covered by sponsors and no tickets being sold for profit.

Notice a theme yet? Tina stays busy. But not just *busy*—Tina stays busy making and shipping work she believes in. It's a healthy compulsion, a desire for deliverables. "I want to be remembered as a person who wasn't afraid to start things," she says.

Many of Tina's ventures began as side projects. The temporary-tattoo business started when her daughter Ella brought home a set of body stickers from another company. They were ugly and didn't apply well, frustrating Tina's strong design ethic. Even though she didn't know much about tattoos, she knew about art and collaboration—so she formed Tattly, the temporary-tattoo company that offers great designs and easy application. Creative Mornings came about through her desire to bring creative collaborators together.

Several years ago, Tina took a sabbatical from her client work to focus on developing her side projects. She's never returned, preferring to work full-time on bringing projects into the world.

Exhibit C: Get in the Box!
Incorporate Structure into a Creative Life

From her home base in Southern California, Elise Blaha is also a compulsive maker of things. Every day, without fail, she makes and shares her art with the world through a website and daily newsletter. This work goes beyond writing and curating; it includes drawing, painting, sewing, knitting, and craft projects of all kinds.

Elise is driven to create. New posts, new photos, and new projects roll out in a steady stream of creativity. One day it's a new set of stamps for sale, another day it's a lesson in gardening. She has posted more than sixty *different kinds* of scrapbooks for all to see, each with its own design and layout—she uses no templates.

Instead, Elise uses the secret that allows "makers" like her to thrive: She clearly defines her projects, and she breaks them down into multiple parts. When she has success with one project, she applies the same format to others. The medium doesn't need to be the same, she told me, but the process for working on them can still be. When she turned twenty-seven, Elise set a goal to create twenty-seven different craft projects using twenty-seven different types of materials. One autumn she baked forty different kinds of bread.

The specifics help, not hinder, Elise's daily creativity. Here's what she says about routine:

> I'm *always surprised about the level of creativity that comes from setting guidelines and boundaries. You would think it's the opposite—that having complete freedom*

*makes everything feel more possible—but in my experi-
ence, that's not the case. I like to say that sometimes to be
the most creative you have to get in a box instead of the
old stand-by thinking outside the box. Often, limitations
force you to think differently about challenges and lead to
better innovations and ideas.*

Lesson: To be creative, don't think outside the box. Make
yourself a box and get into it!*

A Year in the Life

I've long been fascinated by the work of people like Seth,
Tina, and Elise, but sometimes I can't keep up. One time I
was on a trip and wasn't able to read blog posts for ten days.
When I finally connected and downloaded, I had a flood of
content from each of them. Sometimes the act of seeing their
posts is motivation of its own, even if I'm not able to read
each one.

Since it's hard to track, I decided to take a closer look at all
of their work over the course of a year—at least as much as I
could find. For good measure, I included Thomas Hawk, the
manic photographer, in this collection. Here's what I came up
with.

---

* Readers, take note: This concludes all box metaphors for the rest of the book.
You're welcome.

ELISE BLAHA	211 blog posts	11,949 words	Thousands of photos (the exact number is difficult to count)	52 crafts (1 new craft project per week, recorded in detail)
TINA ROTH EISENBERG	972 blog posts	2,209 shared resources	67 cities participating in Creative Mornings	863 Creative Mornings talks posted online
SETH GODIN	365 blog posts (1 per day, no breaks, no exceptions)	76,349 words	3 published books (released on the same day!)	Numerous keynote speeches, interviews, guest writing contributions
THOMAS HAWK	11,697 photos published on Flickr	176 photos published on the blog	141 blog posts	

❂

As I pondered the efforts of Seth, Tina, Elise, and some of their peers, I wasn't sure this intense focus on a certain kind of work qualified as a quest in the classic definition—there were clear endings to particular projects, but not to the overall effort. Nevertheless, I found in these individuals commonalities with people who pursued more traditional quests. They chose to focus on a specific series of outcomes, deriving satisfaction from both the creation process and from sharing it with others. When they finished one piece of work, they moved on to another. They seemed happiest when building a set of interconnected pieces, and they'd structured their lives to allow the work to take preeminence. It was as if they'd chosen a particular kind of life and then changed other circumstances to accommodate it.

The Devotion of Stand-Up Comics

I was surprised to learn that some famous comedians, who've achieved household-name status and banked hundreds of millions of dollars, continue to focus relentlessly on the steady craft of telling jokes onstage. For example, despite appearing on television five nights a week and being viewed by millions, Jay Leno spent the weekends during his final years of hosting *The Tonight Show* getting ready for a smaller performance. Every Sunday, instead of taking it easy, he took the stage at the Comedy and Magic Club in Hermosa Beach, California, for a traditional stand-up routine. Why bother?

Leno sees his routine as a form of self-assessment. If it goes well in the club, he feels OK. If not, he gets worried. "When you work in TV," he told a magazine interviewer, "you get these odd notes on little slips of paper that say you are or aren't doing well with boys between the ages of 9 and 13 or you need to make more cat jokes because the people with cats aren't watching often enough. But if you walk into a 1,500-seat theater and it's packed, you know you are doing fine. If it's only two-thirds full, you know you have some more work to do."

Meanwhile, Jerry Seinfeld, whose estimated worth is $800

million, regularly hops a plane to perform in small clubs throughout the country. Again, why bother? For him, it isn't about reinforcing a success elsewhere. Instead, it's about refinement. "If I don't do a set in two weeks, I feel it," Seinfeld told the *New York Times*. "I read an article a few years ago that said when you practice a sport a lot, you literally become a broadband: the nerve pathway in your brain contains a lot more information. As soon as you stop practicing, the pathway begins shrinking back down. Reading that changed my life. I used to wonder, Why am I doing these sets, getting on a stage? Don't I know how to do this already? The answer is no. You must keep doing it. The broadband starts to narrow the moment you stop."

Both Seinfeld and Leno believe that continually getting onstage without a safety net is key to their ability to thrive. Not only that, but in some ways the journey is the destination—telling jokes and connecting with audiences, however small, is the point itself. According to Seinfeld, the goal is "refining a tiny thing for the sake of it," and he has no plans to stop flying to small cities and putting on unexpected shows in tiny venues.

What do the best stand-up comics have in common? They're driven by obsession. The obsession with continuously refining a small thing can be a quest of its own.

Climb the Right Ladder

Stephen Kellogg has been an independent musician for more than a decade, releasing a dozen albums and playing more than 1,200 concerts. I heard Stephen at a TEDx event, where he shared a story before his performance. When he was a kid, all he wanted to do was play music. He grew up listening to

Bon Jovi and practicing air guitar in his bedroom. Somewhere along the way, the air guitar changed to a real guitar, and Stephen got his first gig.

Times were hard in the beginning, with only a few people coming to concerts that paid almost nothing, but Stephen didn't care. He was a musician! He had the chance to play! At that point in his story he said something that has stayed with me ever since: "It's better to be at the bottom of the ladder you want to climb than the top of one you don't." Compared to a traditional career that might have offered more security, Stephen's struggle to play his own music and cultivate his own fan base made him far happier.

He wrote me later to follow up. When I asked what had changed after 1,200 shows, he said something else I liked: "I've just grown from a boy with an inclination into a man with a focus. It all started with a dream, but then I *followed* that dream. Following the dream made all the difference."

I felt the same way when I started writing. The early work I published wasn't very good (and the work that I *didn't* share was worse), but it still felt good to be doing it. When I woke up in the morning I immediately thought about what I'd work on for the next few hours. At night I'd go to bed thinking about how I could improve the next day. When I started speaking at events, I was terrified—but in a good way. When I got the chance to write my first book, I was thrilled! I, too, felt like I'd found the right ladder to climb, even if I was at the bottom, and even though I had a long way to go.

If you're doing something you love, it doesn't matter that it's challenging. You can keep going for a long time as long as you're motivated—just make sure you choose the right starting point. If you're lucky, as happened with Stephen, your inclination may even become a vocation.

Remember

Some people are motivated primarily by creating and sharing. When they finish one project, they immediately look for another.

Effort can be its own reward if you let it.

To be creative, "get in the box"—create structure and routine that allows you to keep working.

Chapter 11

Joining Forces

In this world, there are things you can only do alone, and things you can only do with somebody else. It's important to combine the two in just the right amount. —HARUKI MURAKAMI

Lesson: SOME ADVENTURES SHOULD BE SHARED.

A funny thing happened to Tom Allen in Yerevan, Armenia. The young British cyclist had been on the road for eight months with barely a break. His friendships with the guys who'd originally left England to see the world with him had suffered, with Tom feeling frustrated that they didn't value exploration as highly as he did. The first friend had returned home after ten weeks to be with his girlfriend, and the other chose to stay behind in Tbilisi, Georgia, a few weeks later.

That's why it was odd, though perhaps also predictable, that Tom would encounter his greatest challenge not in the frozen Alps or even the deserts of Sudan, where he struggled with malaria and disorientation. The *greatest* challenge came through a more ordinary experience: Tom met a girl and fell in love.

Tenny was unlike any girl he'd known in England. Though she hadn't seen much of the world, she shared Tom's curiosity and longing for adventure. Right from the early days of their romance, Tom knew he'd found someone special. Although he'd planned to stay only a few days in Armenia before continuing to Iran, this wasn't a relationship he wanted to let slip away. He found himself adding a day or two to the itinerary, ostensibly to sort out provisions and repairs, and then an extra week because he was so happy to be with Tenny.

As wonderful as falling in love was, meeting Tenny presented Tom with an unavoidable conflict. The girl he loved was in Armenia, a place he was enjoying and where he could possibly stay for a long time. Yet the outside world, starting with the Iranian border sixty kilometers away, was calling to Tom. Was it right to be alone? What do you do when you've promised yourself to go on?

Tom had by then completed the difficult task of obtaining a visa for Iran. The stamp was glued to his passport, growing closer to expiration by the day. After leaving England and riding farther and farther away, the road was all he'd known for the past eight months. Sensing no other option, Tom said good-bye and hit the road again, hoping to be reunited with Tenny at some point in the distant future.

He regretted the decision almost instantly. As he pedaled mile after mile up the steep hills that separated Yerevan from the Iranian border town, he thought about what he was leaving behind. By midafternoon he'd made it all the way to his campsite, but felt racked with guilt over moving on. Finally he did what he should have done before: He chose the girl. "This is for the betterment of my life," Tom said to the handheld camera he'd brought along for the ride. He looked ahead to the border of Iran, then back at the sixty kilometers that separated him from Tenny. Tom turned back and began pedaling, retracing his route to the girl he'd left behind.

The Family Who Doesn't Understand

In the course of all the interviews I did with people undertaking quests, I learned that when it came to support from friends and family, the results were all over the map. Some family members were highly supportive, others merely tolerated the endeavor, and in a few cases family and friends were actively opposed.

John Francis made two big choices that didn't make a lot of sense to everyone else. Choosing to avoid vehicles and walk everywhere was strange enough, but adopting a vow of silence went too far for some people. When he wrote home to his parents to explain his decision, his father got on the next flight to California, more concerned than curious. A friend picked him up at the San Francisco airport and they ran into John walking on the road back near his home. When his father greeted him, John smiled and reached out his hand, but didn't speak. "Damn, son! What is this?" his dad asked, exasperated.

At John's home over the next few days, the older man tried his best to understand. He'd grown to accept the walking, but the vow of silence was beyond comprehension. They had a good visit, but it was clear that John's dad thought something was very wrong. At one point John overheard a phone conversation with his mom, where his dad said he hoped John didn't show up in Philadelphia.

Even a decade later, after John had earned a master's degree from the University of Montana and served as the first-ever silent teaching assistant, his father still didn't get it. "You have to talk," he told him. "What are you going to do with a master's degree? What kind of a job are you going to get? You have to drive a car and you have to talk."

But while John would listen to what his dad had to say, he wouldn't change his mind about the vow of silence for five more years. After graduating from Missoula, he prepared to enter a doctoral program in applied technology. The program was at the University of Pennsylvania, 2,300 miles east. John repacked his day bag, said good-bye to friends, and set out for another long walk on his own.

❂

Alicia Ostarello, who toured the United States to complete her "fifty dates in fifty states" project after a painful breakup, encountered an unexpected challenge early on: her parents. To put it mildly, they were not pleased. Having gathered support from a few friends, Alicia presented the idea to her mom and dad at her birthday dinner. Here's how it went down:

> *We had just poured the wine and said "Salute!" (we're Italian, it's true) and taken sips, when I brought up the topic. My dad actually thought I was kidding. I described what the plan was and how it would work, and instead of telling me it was a horrible idea, he looked puzzled, laughed, and changed the subject. I got the joy of telling him again two days later after my mom told me he thought I was being silly.*

Alicia told me later that while she was grateful for all the support from friends, sponsors, and strangers she met along the way—and also her parents, who eventually came around—in the end she was able to maintain stamina and well-being by focusing inward.

> *I think the best support I had was from myself. I had to know what I truly needed, and what I could live without in order to get everything done in a day. It was an interesting process to simply be my own everything. In a project that was all about dating (and thus in some ways about codependency and the idea that we all want partners) it's ironic to think that one of the reasons I survived was because I was able to support myself.*

If your family doesn't get it, it's hard. But you also need to find people who *do* get it. In the long run, perhaps the best thing you can do is prove it to them. If you're excited about what you're doing, sometimes the opposition will come around, as they did for Alicia.

Juno Kim says that she doesn't expect some members of her family to ever understand. "Is that sad?" I asked. "Well, sometimes," she says. But other people get it, and she still has her family when she goes home.

Family on Bikes

John and Nancy Vogel were two self-described burned-out teachers from Boise, Idaho, raising twin boys and paying a mortgage. The Vogels had a history of pursuing big adventures. Their boys had been born in Ethiopia, where John and Nancy were teaching, and had spent their first four birthdays in a different country each year. After returning to the United States,

Friends on Holiday . . . or Maybe Not

Every year, a tour company called the Adventurists produces a "Rickshaw Run" through India. It's a multistage race conducted entirely in auto rickshaws, with up to forty different teams all hoping to raise money for charity and have a good time along the way.

I heard from several groups that had participated in the Rickshaw Run with good results. One guy described it as the adventure of a lifetime, with shared memories and bonding that he and his rickshaw mates felt would last the rest of their lives.

A member of another group wrote me privately to share a different story. "It was miserable," she said, "And not just from the food poisoning." This group was composed of several women who knew one another online, but hadn't actually met in person before. What a fun story! Except it wasn't. For whatever reason, one of the women didn't click with the others, and the big adventure became a big test in attempting to get along with new acquaintances who weren't really friends.

Lesson: Unless you're feeling especially brave, get to know your companions before agreeing to race a rickshaw with them in India.

John and Nancy's urge to explore exceeded the urge to settle down. The boys' third grade was spent cycling through Mexico and nineteen U.S. states. Fourth grade took place back in Boise, but much of the year was devoted to planning the greatest family excursion yet: a three-year, seventeen-thousand-mile cycling journey from Alaska to the southernmost point of Argentina.

Being on the road for thirty-three months as a family, sleeping in tents every night, and riding through changing climates sounds like a disaster in the making—and there certainly were a lot of challenges. At least three times in the journey, Nancy was ready to pack up and go home. The first crisis came while cycling through the jungles of Central America, passing through tunnels of trees. The scenery was beautiful, but it was hot, humid, and sticky. Nancy did a mental calculation of how much jungle remained: at least six hundred miles. Somehow she kept going, encouraged by the fact that John and the boys weren't struggling as much.

The second crisis came in Peru, where Nancy felt she was locked in a battle of wills with the country itself. "It's a matter of who can hold out longer," she wrote in her journal, "and I suspect Peru has endless amounts of patience."

Once again she kept going, only to face an unexpected challenge in central Argentina, still 1,500 miles and fifty nights of camping away from their destination of Ushuaia. This was nearly the breaking point. Here's how she tells the story:

We pulled into the small town of Zapala as high winds whipped sand into our faces. Tears streamed down my cheeks as my body attempted to wash sand out of my eyes. Communication between my husband and I was unnecessary; he somehow knew I was at my breaking point and another night in the tents would have broken me. We pedaled from hotel to hotel looking for something even remotely within our price range.

After finding a cheap hostel, we dragged our bikes to a spot sheltered from the wind, unlashed all our bags to haul them upstairs, then locked our bikes together before heading up to the dorm room. John and the boys got out the laptop to play video games while I headed to the shower.

Warm water coursed over my body as tears fell from my eyes. I was beyond exhausted. It took everything I had to remain standing in the shower. I thought about what still lay ahead: about all the stories I had heard about the Patagonian winds. Nobody even mentioned northern Argentina, yet this had been the most difficult thing I had ever done.

Was reaching Ushuaia on two wheels important enough to me to continue on? Was accomplishing this goal that I had dedicated so many years of my life to worth the pain it would take to get there? Did I really want to do this?

In the end, I decided I wasn't ready to give up. I was determined I would hate every pedal stroke of the remaining 1,500 miles, but I would do it. I would reach Ushuaia if it killed me.

Interestingly, John and Nancy's twin boys Daryl and Davy had adjusted the quickest to the challenge. They were especially motivated by the goal of becoming the youngest travelers to cross the Americas by bicycle.* An improvised rule specifying "twenty miles per cookie" didn't hurt, either.

Nancy, John, and the boys did make it to Ushuaia, and it didn't kill anyone. One thousand and eighteen days after the Vogels left Alaska, the journey was completed. The boys set the record and many cookies were consumed.

---

*Note to parents: Adam Baker, whose story I told in my previous books, is quick to say that when traveling with kids, they will often adjust quicker than parents will. "When we took our one-year-old overseas," he says, "she was totally fine. We were the ones who had to learn to be flexible."

The family eventually returned to Idaho to regroup yet again. The boys went back to "normal school" and began taking advanced science and math classes. But their bikes and the memory of accomplishment through striving continued to tug at them.

After two years passed, they asked, "When are we going to travel again?" Nancy's answer: "Just say the word."

Back in Armenia

Reunited with Tenny, Tom felt overjoyed. He rented a small apartment and stayed in Yerevan several months, beginning to study the language and find his way around. The journey was far from over, but the break was good.

That's when he added a modification to his plan. Maybe they could do it together! Tom asked Tenny to ride along for part of the journey, and she said yes. Why not?

The two cycled from Yerevan to Tehran, the trip that Tom had nearly made by himself a few months earlier. Once there, they decided to separate again for a time, a decision that was hard but necessary. Tenny's conservative family had grown increasingly suspicious of the strange Western suitor who wanted to take their daughter around the world. Not wanting to completely alienate them, Tom suggested he go on alone and then return for Tenny later—a compromise that she quickly agreed to.

The first time he left Tenny, Tom instantly regretted it. But this time the decision was different. Tenny was a wonderful person and, it seemed, even the love of his life. But Tom realized that he'd made another mistake: Though they loved each other, it wasn't Tenny's dream to cycle the world. A dream can only have one owner, Tom decided. He was committed to Tenny, but his journey wasn't over. They said farewell in Tehran—temporarily, they both hoped—and Tom got back on the bike. From then on, he said, "I would just look forward and try not to think about the what-ifs."

Over the next seven months, Tom returned to the theme of reframing risk and opportunity. "It's about letting a little uncertainty into your life," he said. "Maybe a lot of people will tell me it's stupid to do this . . . but I couldn't just stop because someone told me I had to. I needed to get back on the bike and fight."

Tom journeyed on, through Egypt and the Sudan, contracting malaria and struggling through an extremely challenging environment (there are no bike lanes in Cairo). This part of the trip was the most physically difficult experience he'd ever had, yet he remained hopeful throughout. He was on the road, fulfilling his mission—and he also knew he had someone he loved back in Armenia. Even with the broiling sun during the day and the mosquitoes at night, Tom felt happy.

The next stage of Tom's journey ended in Yemen, a place where few foreigners visit. Tom sat on a beautiful isolated beach and looked back on the year. "Did all of that really happen?" he wondered. He thought about setting out from England, naive but eager. He thought about losing his friends as they made different choices and moved on. He thought about the struggle he'd experienced and the challenges he'd overcome.

Most of all, he thought about Tenny. As beautiful as the beach was in Yemen, his mind remained fixed on the memories of their time falling in love.

He knew the time had come to end the trip. The adventure wasn't over, but part of it had reached its natural conclusion. The first time he turned back for Tenny, he did so consumed with uncertainty, conflicted between following his goal and pursuing someone he cared for deeply. This time he was going back convinced that he'd arrived at a point where it was right to choose love. He'd stared down his insecurities and the border guards of Yemen. He was going home . . . to Armenia.

Tom and Tenny were married in a small ceremony that included Tom's friends from England. Further adventures would await them both, but the trajectory of Tom's life had changed. "I'm no longer the most important person in my life," he said. "Whatever the direction is going to be, it's going to be pursued together."

Remember

If your family or close friends don't understand your dream, you need to find people who do.

Must a dream have only one owner? Not if two or more minds see the world from the same perspective.

Even with the support of others, it's hard to struggle through hardship without sufficient motivation of your own.

Dispatch

STRUGGLE

I flew to Italy and rented a car at Fiumicino airport in Rome. I'd been to Italy several times before and was flying on to a stop in Africa the next day, but first I planned to drive to San Marino, the world's smallest republic, stay for the afternoon, and then drive back. I usually spend at least several days in each country, but San Marino is a small Italian town that managed to achieve diplomatic independence back when countries were still being formed. With a population of just thirty thousand people, it seemed like a fun little place to pop in to for a few hours.

If it didn't turn out to be a total disaster, it probably *would* have been fun.

I was already tired when I arrived at the rental-car counter, far from the arrivals area. Getting to the car itself required another extended hike to an off-site pickup location. As I settled into the vehicle—a tiny European model that felt like a go-kart—the plastic mechanism that opened the driver's side window snapped off. *Oops.* The window was stuck in a permanent position of uselessness: rolled down at least a third of the way, but unable to proceed any further. I decided to head out anyway—what could go wrong?

I set out for San Marino, a destination I thought was about two hours away. These were the days before GPS devices were common, so all I had was a marked-up map from the rental car place.

Two hours must have been the time it took for Formula 1 racers to get to San Marino. Me, I missed an exit and got lost, and then after I finally found the right exit, I got lost again. I went through a series of tollbooths, which probably made sense to Italian travelers but were confusing to an idiot like me. At one I was unable to find a receipt from a previous one, so the gruff toll agent simply issued me a bill for fifty euros. I feigned ignorance and drove away.

Fatigue was kicking in, the result of staying up all night on the overnight flight from Atlanta. At one point my eyes closed for a second and I awoke to find the car scraping the guardrail along the mountain. *Yikes!* With my heart pounding I pulled off at the next exit, looking for a place to park and nap for a while. Unfortunately, this plan didn't work either. It was the middle of the summer and hot. As soon as I turned off the AC, I immediately started sweating. I took my shirt off, then my pants, and tried to sleep in the backseat of the cramped car with my head against the luggage. It worked for about ten minutes.

Giving up, I stepped out of the car and began to put my clothes back on just as a young woman with two children drove by. The kids pointed at me and laughed. ("Oh, hi! Sorry. *Scusi.*") I got back behind the wheel and drove off quickly, frustrated at the lack of sleep and embarrassed by my cameo as the half-naked tourist at the village rest stop.

Somehow I made it to San Marino, four hours after leaving Rome.

I drove back to the airport—four more hours—taking pride in getting to San Marino and learning to pay the tolls properly on the way back. The day's heat wave had turned into a rainstorm. Thanks to my window not rolling up all the way, I spent much of the journey getting soaked.

Thirty miles out from the airport, I ran low on fuel and had to stop at a gas station. Unfortunately, the gas station was unmanned, and the self-pay system wouldn't accept my credit card. Foiled again! I urged the little car on with effort until it limped into the airport. By now the car's side was scraped up from the guardrail encounter, the open window was still frozen in place a third of the way down, a bill of fifty euros for failing to pay the tolls was presumably due at some point, and the gas tank was bone dry.

I wrote a note: "Had some problems with this vehicle."

Returning the keys and note to the drop box, I headed for the terminal. My plane wasn't due to depart until early in the morning, but I looked forward to lying on a bench and resting as well as I could. It had been a crazy adventure, and for once I was glad it was over.

Alas, the terminal had been locked for the night and wouldn't open until six a.m.

Chapter 12

Rebel for a Cause

The most subversive people are those who ask questions.
—JOSTEIN GAARDER

Lesson: FIND WHAT TROUBLES YOU ABOUT THE
WORLD, THEN FIX IT FOR THE REST OF US.

I f something bothered you, what would you do about it? If
your homeland were threatened, would you protest?

How *much* would you protest?

Let's say you were willing to do something. Would you
write to a politician or attend a public meeting? Would you
hold a sign and march?

Most of us have a limit to our activism. If we're troubled by
something, we might ask "What can I do?" but we want the
answer to be easy. We might send a small amount of money or
help spread the word. If we're *really* troubled, we might try to
recruit others to join our cause.

Some people go further.

☻

Howard Weaver was born in Alaska, the son of restless American pioneers who'd moved progressively west from their native Switzerland. Right after college he began his career as a

journalist for the *Anchorage Daily News,* covering the crime beat and following around a couple of known associates of an organized crime family. Unfortunately, his tail-the-target skills were limited, and the mobsters easily tracked him down at home with an unambiguous message: "Don't do that again." After he went to a bar to meet them face-to-face, they laughed at how young he was and bought him a drink.

Howard continued to learn the ropes, getting better at building relationships with sources and being more careful about following mobsters. His first attempt at challenging the voice of the status quo came as the *Daily News* was falling into dire straits. The paper had won the state's first Pulitzer Prize five months earlier, but times were hard and the paper lacked the resources of its main competitor, the *Anchorage Times.* While the *News* sought to present a balanced editorial voice, the *Times* was pro-business to the core. In the minds of many young and progressive-minded journalists, the *Times* wasn't just a competitor. It was the enemy.

Walking away with three friends from the *Daily News,* a good paper that had run out of money, Howard cofounded the *Alaska Advocate,* a scrappy competitor with activist impulses. Beginning with just $5,000—the pooled sum of four $1,250 contributions from the founders—the paper strove to provide an alternative to the big-business voice of the *Times.*

Denied traditional funding from local banks, Howard and his cofounders created a crowdfunding campaign long before Internet fund-raising appeals became common. The youthful team decided to sell unregistered stock, despite not knowing how such a thing worked. Howard went to the stationery store and bought the nicest blank stock certificates he could find, also picking up an embosser for an official seal. The others went door-to-door in Anchorage and other cities to presell subscriptions.

Decades later, their pitch seems amusing and far-fetched: "Would you like to subscribe to a paper that doesn't exist?" But in just a few months they'd acquired a further $10,000 in seed money and were ready to get started. The first issue hit the press with much celebration by the small team.

The *Advocate* had little money after paying expenses at the printing press, and the staff worked for little or no pay. To feed themselves, they attended state functions, scrounging free food at buffets and free drinks at receptions whenever possible.* Despite the limited funding, the team was enthusiastic and worked late into the night. The whole point was to build something, to be part of taking down a giant while armed only with the truth.

The upstart journalists ran free, pushing limits wherever they could. When the *Times* ran a headline saying that the trans-Alaska oil pipeline was safe from sabotage (a questionable claim that was being pushed by big oil), the *Advocate* staff drove to a central area of pipeline and set off a fake explosion, complete with smoke grenades that sent dark plumes into the sky. Nothing happened—which was exactly what they expected. They then claimed that the *Times* story was incorrect, since no one even bothered to check on what seemed like a damaging explosion.

There was no shortage of energy or chutzpah. Still, these antics were more interesting than effective. Howard and his

---

* Howard Weaver: "In Juneau, alcohol was pretty much guaranteed at any event that started after lunch, and sometimes before."

merry pranksters were having fun, but "fighting the man" was a tough business strategy. Moreover, in attacking the *Times* and "big business," they had inadvertently offended most of Alaska's largest companies, which might have been persuaded to support the paper by buying ads. Every week, Howard held a meeting with the bookkeeper to determine which bills could be paid and which should be deferred. The battle to stay afloat came to an end shortly after the *Advocate*'s two-year anniversary. What little money they had was drying up, and the paper folded.

Never Say Die

Fortunately for Howard, the story wasn't over. His old paper, the *Daily News,* had been sold to a California company that was prepared to invest in making it a more serious competitor. The opportunity to provide an alternative media outlet for Alaskans was up for grabs, and Howard returned to the new *Daily News,* where he was now in charge of writing editorials and building a new team. At thirty years old, he once again had in his sights the goal of taking down the establishment newspaper.

For the next thirteen years, Howard and the *Daily News* team worked to produce a newspaper that would provide better news coverage than the *Times,* and eventually surpass them.

Slowly, the tide began to turn. The *Daily News* won a Pulitzer Prize for its coverage of alcohol abuse and suicide among native populations. As the team continued to increase the quality and quantity of local reporting, the *Times* grew more callous—and readers noticed. Every goal has a way to measure success, and in the Great Alaska Newspaper War there was a clear metric: daily subscribers. In the early days, the circulation at the *Daily News* hovered around ten thousand. By the time Howard's team made their second attempt, they had more than twenty thousand readers. The *Times* had always treated the *News* with condescension, but now they had good reason to be worried. All of a sudden, the newspaper world in the mainland United States, which had never cared much about Alaska, was paying attention.

What was special about Alaska? There were essentially two competing stories. The story from the *Times*, the establishment paper, was a story of big oil. Environmental causes were given short shrift or entirely ignored. The plight of native Alaskans, who often struggled with poverty and health problems, was put down to character defects, playing to the latent racism of some in the business community. The other story was one of respect for all Alaskans, and a desire to tell the truth—something you'd expect from a newspaper, but wasn't always common at the *Times*. Howard spoke of his team's values as "an enduring belief that telling the truth would change things. The people can decide for themselves, but you can't lie to the people."

When the *Exxon Valdez* supertanker shuddered into Prince William Sound, disgorging millions of barrels of oil and creating one of the world's worst environmental disasters, the coverage of the two papers was markedly different. The *News* devoted weeks of continual front-page coverage to the disaster and cleanup efforts. But over at the *Times,* the environmentalists were largely ignored, and an editorial stated that the cleanup would be completed in a matter of days. (It took years.) One week after the tanker struck the reef, the *Times* was ready to move on and began shifting coverage to the inner sections of the paper. When Exxon hired thousands of temporary workers in a frantic effort to clean up, the *Times* labeled it a "silver lining . . . an economic bonanza" and "a positive jolt for the economy."

The *Valdez* response further galvanized the team at the *News,* which by then had taken a commanding lead in the newspaper wars. (*The News'* Sunday circulation was seventy-two thousand versus *The Times'* circulation of forty-one thousand.) The *Times* played dirty, buying copies of their own paper to boost the reported circulation numbers, and running puff profile pieces on executives whose firms had agreed to purchase subscriptions in bulk for their employees.

It was a desperate, losing battle for the former giant, and in May 1992 it all came to an end. In a shock to the staff of both papers, the owner of the *Times* finally capitulated. The negotiation took less than a week to complete, with the owner agreeing to close the *Times* and sell its assets to the *News* in exchange for his own editorial page in the *News* for the next three years.

The newspaper war was over. The giant had fallen. Howard and the *Anchorage Daily News* had won.

Doing It All Yourself

As laudatory as Howard's years-long fight for Alaska's citizens was, he at least had the compensation of working with a dedicated team. He drew strength from working closely with others who shared the same pursuit. But what if you're confronting powerful adversaries as an army of one?

That was the case with Miranda Gibson.

A thirty-year-old Australian from the island of Tasmania,

Miranda was troubled by the spread of industrial logging in her homeland's ancient forests. As a child, Miranda had walked through forests thick with hundred-year-old trees that were now being felled at an alarming rate, despite the area's having been nominated as a World Heritage site. Miranda believed there was an imbalance of power in favor of multinational logging companies, which were seemingly unaccountable to local populations. Other people were troubled, too, but few were willing to sacrifice to create real change.

Unlike most of us, Miranda didn't limit her protest efforts to firing off a few emails or donating to an environmental group. She decided to become a living example of activism, doing whatever she could to bring awareness to the cause and stop the industrial logging. Her means of protest? She climbed to the top of a sixty-meter-high eucalyptus tree . . . and told the world she'd stay there until the problem was solved.

❂

What's life like in the top of a eucalyptus tree? Well, the environment is fairly active. An installed platform provides a vantage point to observe a bustle of activity. You can look out at the fading light of the day and see Tasmanian devils causing trouble on the ground floor. Owls begin to awaken and say hello to their neighbors. Most of the inhabitants of the forest aren't accustomed to sharing space with humans, but after you stay for months, they get used to you.

Outside visitors come and go, making their way up to say hello through an improvised pulley system. Thanks to the wonders of modern technology, supportive messages arrive from all time zones.

But the visitors, the messages, and even the noise from the owls are blips on a continuous radar of monotony. Mostly, there's a lot of solitude. "Sometimes it gets lonely up here," Miranda told me by email in what seemed like the understatement of the century.

Miranda set up camp in the tree and began chronicling the activities of the forest with a worldwide audience. Her actions brought quick short-term relief. The loggers, not wishing to wage a moral battle with a young woman living in a tree and receiving global attention, left the immediate area.

But how long was she prepared to stay? The goal wasn't just to get the loggers to disperse, but to make it illegal or impossible for them to return. In other words, this wasn't a short-term project. Miranda stayed in the tree for weeks, and then months. The seasons changed and she was still there. An entire year passed, and she hadn't moved.

Miranda corresponded with me around Day 400 in her protest. She'd recently celebrated her second Christmas high above the earth.

I wanted to know more, so I asked her if we could speak by phone. "Even better," she said. Miranda is equipped with perhaps the world's only Wi-Fi hot spot at the top of a hundred-year-old tree, so we arranged a Skype session. "Why do this?" I asked, through a surprisingly strong video connection. "Why you?"

"This is what I knew I could do," she said. "Nothing else seemed to get attention."

When Miranda climbed the tree and set up "camp" at the top, she definitely got attention. Even better, the loggers continued to stay away.

Worth Living For

One online commenter wondered about Miranda Gibson's motivations: "Is she doing this to make up for something lacking in her personal life?" But you could ask the same thing about anyone devoted to a cause. Who's to say why anyone cares about anything? If you're willing to spend a year living in a tree, you have to really believe in something.

When I was a kid, I sat on the back row at a lot of dramatic late-night church services.

Often the preacher or evangelist would tell a story about our fellow believers in Russia, China, or Cuba (Communist countries were seemingly interchangeable) being surrounded by soldiers outside a church and forced to recant their faith or risk execution.

No matter the details, the story was always followed with a challenge: "Would you be willing to die for your faith?"

Looking back, it's easy to see how limited this question was. What's truly worth dying for? It's difficult to know for sure— rarely does anyone get a say in how they die and whether it's for some kind of cause. Most of us die whenever the time comes, whether we're prepared to make a statement or not.

And yet, every single day, each of us gets to answer a far more interesting question: What's worth *living* for? If you could only pursue one thing, what would you craft a life around and do every day? And what if real sacrifice was involved . . . would you stick with it?

Dying for something is heroic. In the rare case when it happens, you go down in a blaze of glory, clutching to your morals or cause. Nice work if you can get it. Years later, Brad or Angelina will play you in the movie.

But living for something can be mundane—and therefore far more sacrificial, because seldom does anyone else notice. You just go on living, beating the drum for the thing you've chosen to value above all else. Genuinely living for something, day after day, is much more valuable than looking for the blaze of glory at the end.

So what do you think—what's truly worth living for?

"Maybe People Just Don't Know"

A wildlife veterinarian from Canada, Helene Van Doninck is on a one-woman campaign to convince hunters to switch to non-lead ammunition. Every year during hunting season, she sees a number of bald eagles who've been poisoned from swallowing lead ammunition in hunted game meat. These eagles are a national treasure and an endangered species, but many die after being exposed to the lead.

Helene believes this is entirely preventable, so she has been working intensely to convince hunting groups and local communities to adopt resolutions urging the use of non-lead ammunition. She launched the crusade after a difficult week where she watched four eagles die from poisoning. At first she was angry, but then she realized: "Maybe people just don't know there's a better way."

Helene's attitude is that this is her own quest and she doesn't need permission from anyone to pursue it. The biggest challenge she faces comes from hunters who think she's advocating for an end to hunting, which isn't the case at all. "I just want people to understand that there's an alternative," she wrote. "Sometimes I meet people who don't get it, but after a while I decided, screw it, I'm a volunteer and no one can fire me."

365 Charities

After working in the nonprofit world for fifteen years, including overseas stints in Sudan and Cambodia, Stephanie Zito was feeling discouraged. During her time with different organizations she'd seen a lot of good work and hopeful stories, but there was also a lot of bureaucracy.

Restless, she embarked on a mini-quest as a challenge to her own disbelief. For an entire year, every day she'd learn about a new person, project, or organization that was making the world a better place. She'd also make a $10 donation toward the cause, and whenever possible, write about what happened with the money. She called the project #Give10.

The financial cost for #Give10 was moderate (a total of $4,260: $10 for every day during a Leap Year, and an extra $600 in "readers' choice" donations three times during the year). Even on a nonprofit salary, it wasn't terribly difficult to come up with the money. What took work was finding the people, projects, or organizations to support.

It turned out that giving away $10 to a different recipient every day was surprisingly hard. Stephanie was working throughout Asia for much of the project, flying back and forth to Bangkok every week from her home in Phnom Penh, and often further afield to Mongolia or elsewhere. To ensure she didn't get behind, she made a rule that she wouldn't go to bed at night until she had made the donation. Some nights she'd be up until midnight in Cambodia or Thailand, straining not to fall asleep in front of the laptop. But each morning she was glad she had found someone and kept going. Taking it day by day, making it a habit, and telling the world about it were all helpful in ensuring she'd stick it out.

The response from friends and followers who read Stephanie's daily posts was interesting. Friends were supportive, as you might expect. Some followers said later that they felt guilty while reading the updates, because they weren't making any donations of their own. More positively, several people wrote to ask if it would be OK to start their own #Give10 projects and contribute for a month or even a year. One woman created a #Give25 project for her twenty-fifth birthday. Another person was quitting smoking, and decided to put the money they were saving toward charitable giving. Once in a while, someone would learn about a cause or organization through Stephanie's posts, and they'd decide to support it, too.

The quest wasn't only about giving; it was also about discovery. Looking beyond the big charities, Stephanie hoped to find lesser-known organizations, projects, and people that needed help. She supported a project called Liter of Light that helps slum villages create their own solar lighting through recycled plastic bottles. She gave to a five-year-old boy in Rochester, New York, who sold paintings online to raise money for medical research. She helped build a playground in the Philippines. Every day was a new story and a new chance to learn.

What Bothers You?

If you're trying to find your own quest, you may find it helpful to ask yourself a few questions. Some people find their quests by focusing on *passions* and *interests*—something they love to do or parts of the world they want to explore.

If that doesn't work, though, try a different approach. Instead of asking what excites you, ask what bothers you. There is no shortage of problems in the world, but which one are you most troubled by? What problem are you able to do something about?

Miranda Gibson was troubled by industrial logging in Tasmania, so she climbed a tree and received global attention for the cause. Helene Van Doninck found her answer by focusing on hunting in her native Nova Scotia.

What bothers *you*?

❂

Four hundred and forty-nine days after Miranda climbed the tree, she had to come down . . . urgently. The problem wasn't a lack of commitment or a change of heart—the problem was a bushfire that had burned to within a kilometer of Miranda's tree. Nearly a year and three months had gone by since she first laid claim to the treetop and adopted a strange lifestyle of Skyping with journalists by day and sleeping with the stars at night. All of a sudden, it was all over.

During the entire time Miranda was in the tree, she wore a safety harness. When she came down, she continued wearing it until someone pointed out that it was no longer needed. A bustle of reporters and photographers awaited her arrival, and she sat by the tree holding the rope for a long time.

Finally she concluded that she'd proven her point and walked away. After spending a year in the tree, Miranda felt confident that the logging companies wouldn't dare move back in. If they did, she'd be ready and willing to do it again. Like the child who saves a single starfish on the beach, Miranda had saved a forest.

Remember

—— —— ——

Having an enemy or opponent (even an imaginary one) can keep you focused.

What's worth living for? matters more than *What's worth dying for?*

Understanding what bothers you is just as important as understanding what excites you.

Chapter 13

The Long Road

I am a slow walker, but I never walk back.

—ABRAHAM LINCOLN

Lesson: THE MIDDLE OF A QUEST CAN BE THE
HARDEST PART. DON'T GIVE UP TOO SOON!

It was the largest symphony ever composed. The list of instrumentation reflected an ambition to produce nearly all the sounds of Western orchestra music for the past century. In addition to the usual requirements—a wide range of woodwinds, brass, strings, and percussion—the composer had called for a litany of lesser-known instruments. Six sets of timpani were required, four to be stationed offstage. Five choirs would assemble onstage, including one children's choir. A number of unusual requests had to be fulfilled, including a thunder machine and a "bird scarer," which operated pretty much as described. Nearly two hundred instrumentalists would contribute their efforts to the two-hour production.*

It was called the Gothic Symphony. Because of its girth,

---

*A bird scarer is available in many forms, with convenient online delivery provided by Amazon.com or your favorite local bird shop. Also available: a bird buzzer, a bird wailer, and a bird screecher "with over 90 constantly changing sounds."

and perhaps because its composer, Havergal Brian, didn't boast the same one-name fame as Beethoven or Bach, the Gothic had only been performed a few times. In fact, it hadn't been performed at all in the past thirty years, and never outside of the United Kingdom.

Gary Thorpe, the manager and DJ of a classical music station in Brisbane, Australia, had seen the 1980 performance of the Gothic in London's Royal Albert Hall. He'd left the production feeling ecstatic. "Few people understood twentieth-century classical music," Gary told me. "They think of it as tuneless and boring. But it's not! It's some of the most exciting music that's ever been composed."

The performance in London inspired a dream: to produce the symphony in his hometown. With a population of nearly three million people, Brisbane isn't small. Nevertheless, when you think of classical music, chances are you think first of places such as Vienna, Rome, and Berlin—not a seaside city in faraway Australia.

"I wanted to show that Brisbane had the talent to put this on," Gary continued. "I felt it would attract the attention of the whole world if we could do it right."

The only problem was getting it done.

The sheer coordination of talent and resources was overwhelming, and, time after time, he failed. The first attempt failed for lack of an orchestra, the second for lack of funding, the third for lack of a suitable venue. The fourth time would be the charm, Gary thought—until it became clear that there was no way they could find enough choristers.

These failures happened over twenty years. Each attempt required selling the vision over and over, gathering a new team and trying to convince skeptical venue managers that this time it would work. "I just kept on pitching the Gothic to whoever would listen," Gary said. "I've been told it's not worth it, it's not a masterpiece, it's too difficult. There are reasons why it's only been performed four times in history."

The Gothic symphony was said to be cursed—a description that Gary laughed off until he spent twenty years trying to produce it.

"The hardest aspect from my point of view was to maintain the belief in the value of doing this symphony," he said.

The Leader Requires a Team (and the Team Requires a Leader)

Gary gives generous credit to those who contributed to the massive effort required to bring together hundreds of performers for a herculean symphony. He encourages others to put together a team as early as possible. "Try to involve as many talented and capable people in your quest as you can," he wrote me. "It can be lonely and dispiriting doing everything yourself."

No doubt this is true, and Gary certainly couldn't do everything himself—someone had to operate the bird scarer. But Gary was the tireless visionary who led the charge, year after year and through repeated failures. Without the team, the effort would have been in vain. Without the leader, there would have been no effort.

The long, slow grind of working toward something is all about loving the process. If you don't love the process, the grind is tough.

The grind is also a dangerous time. It's when you're tempted to give up, call it a day, or at least cut corners. Steven Pressfield, author of a dozen books, says, "The most important thing about art is to work. Nothing else matters except sitting down every day and trying." So, too, for a quest. The most important thing is continuing to make progress.

Another year passed, and Gary regrouped for his fifth attempt at producing the Gothic Symphony. Once again he gathered a team and found a promising conductor who was willing to contribute his efforts. Alas, when it came to negotiating dates with a festival coordinator, the team discovered an irreconcilable conflict with the dates. The curse had struck again!

Nine months later, Gary went back to work on the Gothic yet again. This time, a documentary filmmaker who'd been filming Gary's efforts to bring the Gothic to Brisbane chose to give up her objectivity. After watching Gary get stuck time and time again, Veronica Fury stepped in and officially joined the team. More good news arrived in the form of a grant for $25,000—not all that the group needed to produce the massive symphony, but a great start. An enthusiastic choir leader from Sydney also decided to join the cause, and everyone was feeling cautiously optimistic.

Alas (you knew this was coming), something went wrong again. The great choir leader from Sydney dropped out, leaving the production without a crucial component. One step forward, one step back. They canceled the booking at the performance hall. Everyone agreed that the project needed a rest.

❂

One year later, Gary and the rest of the Brisbane team regrouped once more. This time, they were committed to seeing it through. "It's the Mount Everest of classical music!" Gary said. "We've come to base camp a few times but always had to retreat." (Reminder: You might be excited about something even if it's not interesting to other people, and you must believe in your project even if no one else does.)

After six failed attempts in twenty-eight years, it seemed that things were finally coming together. They had the conductor, a bare-bones budget, and a ragtag band of choristers that had been assembled from across the country. And then, yet another crisis arose when the venue managers called to cancel the booking. Maybe they'd heard rumors of the project's repeated failure, or maybe they just weren't thrilled about sorting out the logistics for a massive orchestra and four separate choirs. Whatever the reason, they suddenly developed cold feet.

Was it failure yet again? No—in Gary's words, it was a call to arms. The filmmaker looked at Gary and said, "You must go in there and secure that booking."

But Gary couldn't go. After nearly three decades of harassing everyone in Brisbane, his appeals would likely be met with polite smiles and demurrals. The Gothic, Gary said, was the best-known musical piece in the city . . . that had never been performed.

Gary went to the venue with the rest of the group, but waited in the lobby while everyone else went up to the meeting. For forty minutes he paced back and forth, unable to do anything. Having waited twenty-eight years, only to be threatened with losing the venue just as everything else was coming together, he felt powerless and intensely frustrated.

The rest of the group finally emerged, and as they did they

flashed a thumbs-up sign. They'd persuaded the venue managers to retain the booking!

All obstacles had been cleared. Gary's day job was at a classical music station, and he took to the airwaves to push the ticket sales. "It's a once-in-a-lifetime opportunity!" he reminded his listeners.

With so many performers, from the hundreds of instrumentalists to the quartet of choirs, rehearsals were a challenge. Mastering the material was hard enough on its own—presenting it in unified fashion, with every detail in place as written by the composer long ago, was even tougher. Still, the big day finally came. There was no more time to prepare, and no going back. Game on!

How to Pay for Your Adventure

Most people who read this book have a certain amount of disposable income. You may not think of yourself as rich, but you're able to buy things you like from time to time. More important, you're able to pay for *experiences*. Most quests are about taking action rather than acquiring "stuff"—and most actions can be quantified into a time-and-money model where you figure out exactly what it costs, then you calculate how to pay for it.

When it comes to travel, I've learned that there are very few places on the planet that require breaking the bank to get to for a few days. Even the most expensive parts of the world can be reached for $2,500 or less. If that sum seems exorbitant, just think of it as $2 a day for three and a half years, or a

Road as Life

Travel can be disorienting and unstable. You're out there in an unfamiliar place, doing new things and adopting different patterns. Sometimes, though, travel itself can provide a welcome sense of motion. Juno Kim, who left a steady job in South Korea to see the world, said that travel provided her with a foundation:

One of my theories about traveling is that it helps us to be in a stable condition. There are so many reasons to travel: for holiday, getaway, challenge, adventure, hiding . . . and we wish to get some answers at the end. To get a precise answer about myself, I need to be in that stable condition; I need to be happy and I need to know myself. And the best way to find those two is travel, at least it was for me.

Just as you should define your own goals and decide for yourself what constitutes success, consider your own definition of stability. Is it a safe job and comfortable home of your own, or is it something else? Do you always have to choose between foreign and familiar, or can you mix it up? Juno found stability by leaving behind what was considered a much more stable lifestyle. She found her "stable condition" far from her native land.

bit less than $7 a day over one year. Can you save that much? If so, you can go anywhere.*

---

* Read more on the $2/day experiment at ChrisGuillebeau.com/3x5/your-one-place.

"It Costs What Life Costs": How Different People Funded Their Projects

I asked everyone whose story is told in this book how much their project or quest cost, and how they were able to pay for it. Responses varied considerably.

Juno Kim, the twenty-seven-year-old South Korean woman, originally took her savings with her and planned to live off that money as long as it lasted. But four years and twenty-four countries later, she's actually *increased* her savings, thanks to her work as a freelance writer and photographer.

Scott Young, who taught himself the MIT computer science curriculum in one year, spent five days a week learning full-time, one day a week resting, and one day a week working on a business to pay the bills. Because he possessed only a few hours to devote to moneymaking efforts, he had to make those hours count. Fortunately, he'd started the business as a busy undergraduate student, so he was used to focusing on the right tasks instead of surfing the Internet all day. Despite Scott's efficiency, the MIT project required some trade-offs. "My goal during that year was to just keep the business running. As a result I didn't have much time to do business development. I didn't make any significant business expansions or improvements during that time."

Ron Avitzur worked on his graphing calculator project for free, sneaking into Apple headquarters early in the morning and staying until night. He lived frugally and ate cheap meals. "I wasn't a big spender," he told me. "But it also helped that we worked all the time."*

---

*After the secretly developed software successfully shipped on every Apple

Mark Boyle, a man from Bristol, England, who chose to live without money for more than a year, wrote in to say that his project conveniently had zero financial costs. However, that didn't mean he was alone. After a difficult first two months, as he learned to adapt to life without money, his mutual support network grew. "The more you help people unconditionally," he said, "the more they help you back in the same spirit, but without any of the formality that money inflicts on us."

When going on a big trip, most questers chose to pay their own way, in the belief that it was their dream and they wanted to fund it themselves. However, Matt Krause, who walked across Turkey by himself, had a different idea: "I funded half of the trip with Kickstarter, and would highly recommend that people doing something outlandish in life give others the chance to participate in it. If you're going to do something outlandish, there are a probably a lot of people who would like to do it, too, but don't for various reasons."

Perhaps Meghan Hicks, whose story is told more in chapter 16, put it best in describing how she pays for a lifestyle oriented around the outdoors: "I don't think I can put a price tag on it, but it costs what life costs. My boyfriend and I choose to live a simple, frugal life so that we can do things we are passionate about."

---

computer, Ron spent some time overseas as a research fellow and then started his own company. He continued to develop the graphing calculator.

Show Me the Money

I asked, and they answered. Here are the costs of several of the quests featured in the book. All figures were provided by respondents, and in some cases they are estimates.

NAME	QUEST	TIME	MONEY
Tom Allen	Bike from England to Iran	7½ months	$4,500
Nate Damm	Walk across America	8 months	$4,500
Travis Eneix	1,000 days of tai chi	1,000 days	$0
Josh Jackson	See a baseball game at every MLB stadium	28 years	$100 per stadium
Jia Jiang	100 Days of Rejection Therapy	100 days	$0
Julie Johnson	Train her own guide dog	14 months	$1,500
Steve Kamb	"Epic Quest of Awesome"	3+ years	$40,000*
Juno Kim	Travel to 20+ countries	3+ years	$27,000
Matt Krause	Walk across Turkey	8 months	$10,000
Sasha Martin	Cook a meal from every country	3 years	$18,000 ($500-per-month grocery budget)

NAME	QUEST	TIME	MONEY
Alicia Ostarello	50 dates in 50 states	9 months	$25,825
Gary Thorpe	Produce largest symphony in history	28 years	$280,000†
The Vogel Family	Bike from Alaska to Argentina	33 months	$66,000
John "Maddog" Wallace	Run a marathon in more than 99 countries	10+ years	$250,000
Scott Young	Master in 1 year the MIT curriculum	12 months	$1,500
Stephanie Zito	Give to 365 charities	12 months	$4,260

*Includes tuxedo rental in Monaco and all living expenses.
†Bird scarer not included.

Adventure Savings Fund

"To go anywhere, save $2 a day"—this was the headline for a group project I hosted on my blog. The concept is that there is nowhere in the world you can't visit if you save even a small amount of money over time.

You can apply the concept to any quest, adventure, or project (not just a trip!). Start by answering a few questions:

• What is the cost of my proposed quest or project?

- How long will it take me to save this amount of money?
- Is there any other way to get the money (crowdfunding, selling something, extra work, robbing banks)?
- Do I need to wait to start until I have all the money?
- If getting the money will be difficult, is there a way to reduce the cost?

Example: Visit Antarctica

Getting to Antarctica is fairly expensive, at around $5,000 to $10,000 per person depending on the specific trip. But even that somewhat imposing cost can drop radically if you're willing to be flexible. Every week during the main season of visiting Antarctica (November to March), ships leave from the south of Argentina with a few extra berths. If you don't need to know exactly when you'll be back, the cost can be as much as 40 percent less.

Solution Number One: Save a lot of money and pay full fare.
Solution Number Two: Save less money and hang out in Argentina, waiting to pounce on a berth.

SELECTED SAVINGS RATES

If you can save even more than $2 a day, you can probably get wherever you need to go sooner.

$25/day = $9,125/year
$10/day = $3,650/year
$5/day = $1,825/year
$2/day = $730/year

The Fake Marathon

As I read up on other people's experiences with quests and journeys, I found one story that was truly bizarre. Kip Litton, a middle-aged dentist from Michigan, was also a dedicated marathon runner who set out on a quest to run fifty marathons. He trained every day before treating patients and spent much of his free time on weekends flying to races. So far, so good, right?

Except as other runners began looking at his claims, examining his posted run times against publicly available photos and other data, something seemed wrong. Litton always started a couple of minutes behind all the other runners, then disappeared from the course for more than an hour. He reappeared at the finish line, usually at the front of the pack but wearing different clothes.

Finally, one of the other runners leveled a charge: At best, the middle-aged dentist was exaggerating many of his race times. At worst, he was making it all up. It wasn't just a question of taking a few minutes off the clock, as bad as that would be. According to allegations leveled at him on forums and blog posts, then later investigated and reported in the *New Yorker,* Litton had taken cheating to a whole new level, even inventing a race in Wyoming that never happened.

The "West Wyoming Marathon" had its own website, complete with extensive listings and race times of fictitious runners. On MarathonGuide.com, a popular site that chronicles details of different races, several reviews appeared. "Great race!" one contestant enthused. "A runner's dream!" exclaimed another. It was an amazing effort . . . for something that didn't exist, and in support of a goal that mattered only to the person who created it.

As strange as the fake marathon was, Kip Litton didn't fabricate *everything*. He really was a runner, he'd ran marathons in the past, and by all accounts he was a nice guy with no complaints lodged against his Michigan dental practice. Somewhere along the way, though, he started looking for shortcuts in his quest. Perhaps the problem was the goal itself. Instead of just running fifty marathons—an impressive feat on its own!—Litton's goal was to run each marathon at a sub-3:00 pace. (This is also known as "very fast.")

No one knows exactly when or why Litton began fabricating details of his quest, but one theory is that the time-based goal of sub-3:00 was simply too difficult for him. The lure of accomplishment grew to exceed the reality of completing the task at hand, so he started cutting corners. Once he'd knocked down his actual time a few minutes with no immediate consequences, perhaps it was just too tempting to fabricate an entire race.*

❂

The story of Kip Litton is essentially the dark side of a quest. What happens when you can't achieve the goal, yet still feel immense pressure to claim victory? I was toward the end of my own quest when I read Litton's story, and it caused me to wonder if I'd ever feel tempted to make things up. In my case, the goal of visiting every country was just a personal dream for nearly the first half. After people started following along,

---

*An extended analysis of Kip Litton's fictitious marathon quest was published by Mark Singer. The author of the article, as well as many race directors, concluded that the entire quest was fictitious. Attempts to contact Kip Litton to respond to this section of the book were ignored.

my life became a lot busier and I often had to cancel trips at the last minute due to visa or flight complications, which then threw other plans into disarray.

It certainly would have been easier if I suddenly didn't have to get to Saudi Arabia or Somalia—and I might have rationalized that no one would notice—but my quest was never about proving something to others. It was always about proving something to myself.

I don't think the lesson is to be a better person than the dentist who faked a marathon quest. For reasons known only to him, it seems he just got carried away somehow. The lesson is to know your own motivations. That way, you'll keep going even if no one else cares.

Walking Across Turkey

The middle of a quest can feel like a long run (hopefully one that you're not fabricating). Later on, you'll look back on some of the experiences and ask yourself, "Did those things really happen?" But sometimes, on the road or in the wilderness, you look back at the life you left behind and ask yourself the same question.

At a pace of sixty miles a week, forty-two-year-old Matt Krause walked across Turkey. His journey took six months, ending at the Iranian border, and Matt was a true pilgrim. Every day he walked an average of nine miles: a steady pace, but one that allowed him plenty of time to soak up the experience. Why walk?

"I walk," he wrote in his journal, "to challenge myself to be less afraid of the world." He continued:

Walking is me submitting to the world. When I walk, my speed is slow, and my range is limited. I have little choice but to accept the world as it exists in front of me. Walking is a great way to see the country and meet its people, but I could see the country and meet its people by bus. Walking turns this trip into a personal pilgrimage, a way for me to practice submission to the world mile after mile, day after day, week after week, month after month.

One day Matt decided to check in at a *jandarma* post, a local security checkpoint that kept the peace in rural areas far from bigger cities. He'd heard that *jandarma* posts were essentially the travel agencies of rural Turkey, offering free resting points and the opportunity to receive advice on routing. But when he stopped in to say hi, he received more than just a place of rest. The commander ordered his chef to prepare a hot breakfast, which was delivered within minutes. After they talked over tea for an hour, exchanging life stories, the commander gave him the name of a friend in the next town. When Matt left the guard station, he had a spring in his step and a package of cheese sandwiches that the chef had whipped up to send along for his lunch.

The rest of the day, Matt walked along a two-lane road by the side of the mountains near the Göksu River. The beauty of the environment was overwhelming. In some ways, it reminded him of his old home in the Pacific Northwest. Back in Seattle, though, nobody gave him a free breakfast when he asked for directions, and folks didn't make a habit of dropping in on strangers for an hour-long chat. *The people I know in America don't understand the rest of the world,* Matt thought.

If I can at least show them a small part of it, maybe that will help.

That night Matt made it to the village he'd mentioned to the guard post commander, and he remembered the recommendation he'd been given. The guy's name was Hoca, and conveniently for Matt, it turned out that Hoca owned a small restaurant. In the time-honored hospitality tradition of much of the world, when Matt introduced himself and mentioned their mutual friend, he was instantly welcomed.

Once again, a plate of food appeared, and a dozen cups of tea were shared. Another patron of the restaurant showed up and offered Matt a place to stay back at his apartment. Matt's rule for the journey was "no free car rides"—the whole point of his mission was to *walk* across Turkey. But Matt gladly accepted this kind stranger's offer of a couch to sleep on. They headed back to the apartment and spent an evening watching Turkish matchmaking TV and sitting around the fire.

The next morning Matt thought back on the day's experiences, from the scrambled eggs and cheese sandwiches he'd received at the guard post to the evening spent at Hoca's restaurant and at the stranger's apartment. At no point in the process was a bill presented. Everyone was surprised to see a foreigner traveling independently through Turkey (and on foot!), and new friendships were forged all around.

Later, Matt reflected on his old cubicle job in Seattle. "I hated that job," he told me. "Every day I dreamed of getting away." Now that he'd escaped for the open road in Turkey, those days back home seemed so far away.

Matt said good-bye to his hosts and walked another nine miles toward Iran. The journey continued.

Back in Brisbane

One week before the symphony was set to be performed for the first time in twenty-eight years, Gary Thorpe stood at the arrivals hall of the Brisbane airport with a sign that simply read "Gothic." Fans and friends of the composer were coming in from England and elsewhere, excited for the big debut. Everyone else was excited, too, but they were also nervous.

On the big night, having waited nearly three decades, Gary worried about being late. With everything else that had gone wrong until then, it wouldn't have surprised him to have been shut out of the concert hall, or delayed by a massive traffic jam, or struck by some other disaster. But then a strange thing happened: Everything went according to plan. The show went off without a hitch, ending with an extended standing ovation.

The choirmaster, who'd worried she was making a career-ending move by agreeing to manage the ragtag band of choristers, was ecstatic. "We absolutely nailed it," she said. "We did it. It was sensational to be up there onstage. We were so proud!"

Gary called it a masterpiece. The reviews concurred, with the international press calling it "a triumph beyond all expectation."

❂

Why produce the largest symphony of all time? You do it for the same reason John F. Kennedy offered for visiting the moon—not because it's easy, but because it's hard. In the case of the Gothic Symphony, you do it because it's enormous. You bring it to a city not known for producing massive works of art. London, Berlin, or New York hadn't been able to produce the symphony in thirty years. Why should a small city in Queensland, Australia, take on such a project? That's the point—to do what you're not supposed to do. To do it because it is overwhelming, because it is ridiculous.

It took twenty-eight years and many failed attempts, but the curse of the Gothic Symphony was broken.

Remember

The middle of the quest can be the hardest part. As long as you still believe in the goal, don't stop!

By saving as little as $2/day for just a few years, you can go anywhere in the world.

If your quest relies on external recognition, be sure you have sufficient internal motivation as well.

Chapter 14

Misadventures

Every step gets him closer to greatness . . . or disaster.
—JODY FELDMAN

Lesson: CHOOSE YOUR FAILURES, AND HAVE
THE RIGHT KIND OF DISASTERS.

Mark Boyle set out from Bristol, England, with a spring in his step and a pack on his back. A large group of well-wishers saw him off, including friends, family, and even a guy playing a conch shell. It was big fanfare for a huge undertaking. Mark wasn't just walking from England to India, as impressive as that would be on its own. Mark had a greater quest in mind: He wanted to make the whole trek without spending a single dollar, pound, or rupee. He wanted to travel the world without money, relying on the kindness of strangers and random events of the universe to provide.

Mark expected the journey to take two and a half years. In England he was a local celebrity, having received an abundance of publicity before the big departure, and he preached the gospel of extreme frugality to anyone who'd listen. Friends helped out as he roamed southward, and even strangers chatted him up throughout Ireland and Britain. Mark was quick to explain that he wasn't a freeloader; he was an adherent of the "freeconomy movement," where skills are traded in exchange for food, clothing, or shelter. "I will be offering my skills to people [along the way]," he told the BBC. "If I get food in return, it's a bonus."

Unfortunately, the plan quickly fell apart as he left his native shores. Living without money was tough. Crossing the channel to France, Mark quickly discovered that his schoolboy French had deserted him. He felt unable to speak a single word. Even worse, he was unable to communicate anything about his mission, and the values that had inspired him to leave home were not as universally understood as he'd hoped. In England his mission was seen as interesting and honorable, but in France people considered him a beggar. He hadn't even cleared the next border before deciding his quest was over. Turning around and heading back to England, the journey that was supposed to take two and a half years was over in a single month.

Fail Quickly

John Lasseter, one of the founders of Pixar, says that "Every one of our films was the worst motion picture ever made at one time or another." At the studio that brought *Toy Story* and other hit movies to the world, the creative team embraces mistakes and failure, with an emphasis on making the mistakes as quickly as possible. As soon as they identify the mistakes, they're then able to fix them—but the point is to not shy away from the initial failure.*

When I conducted the research for *The $100 Startup,* I spent a lot of time analyzing the unconventional successes of many new business owners. The book was well received, but

---

* "Be Wrong as Fast as You Can," *New York Times Magazine,* January 6, 2013.

the number one question I heard at the first public readings was "What about all the failures? Don't most businesses fail?" At first I was caught off guard by the question. No, most new businesses don't fail, and if you take the right steps in the beginning, the odds of success go way up. Then I realized that some people are simply obsessed with failure—or at least they have a *general expectation* that a new project will more likely meet with failure than success.

Struggling for the right answer to the question, I learned to dissect the idea of failure more closely. If you start a business and it operates successfully for a number of years, then winds down as you move on to something else, is that a failure? What if you start a business and the initial idea doesn't work, but then you pivot to something more marketable—is that a failure? I'd argue that both of these common experiences are successes.

When to Keep Going and When to Stop

In pursuing any difficult project, sooner or later the thought will pop into your head: Should I quit? You might be tempted to banish this self-doubt immediately, forbidding it to ever make an appearance again. Full speed ahead!

And you might be right in doing that. Nothing worth doing is ever easy.

However, there may be other times when the right choice is to redirect, or perhaps stop entirely. Which is which—and how do you know?

Finding a satisfactory answer to this problem is critical, and not everyone's answer will be the same. Nevertheless, there are a few factors to keep in mind when evaluating this tough question.

1. **Motivations.** Why did you begin this project in the first place? What drove you to challenge yourself? Presumably, there were many different options you could have chosen for your quest or adventure, but for some reason, you settled on this one. Are you still driven by the same motivations?

2. **Long-term happiness.** Short-term relief and long-term happiness can be very different things. When Nate Damm was slogging across West Virginia, getting rained on and placing one sore foot in front of the other, he could have found short-term relief by checking into a motel and calling a friend to pick him up. For at least a few hours, he might have been happier with that course of action. But he was smart enough to realize that the quick fix wouldn't last for the long term. Sooner or later, he'd be kicking himself for not continuing with his quest. Faced with this realization, he kept going.

3. **Rewards.** Can you create a small reward at the end of your day, or at the completion of an important task? After passing through customs and immigration hundreds of times around the world, I initiated a mental game of guessing how long it would take to clear the process each time. Upon landing I'd think through the variables: *Do I already have a visa? How long will the queue take? Am I expecting anything abnormal about the procedures?* This "immigration gamification" was oddly entertaining, if only to me.

4. **Engagement of others.** Sasha Martin, who prepared a meal from every country while living in Oklahoma, said that she felt motivated by the fear of failure—even driven by it at times. She explained that she was sensitive to letting down other people who believed in her. "My family

and friends are always in the back of my mind, and that knowledge keeps me strong, especially on days when I'd rather do nothing else than take a time machine back to the simple, free days before I began the project," she said.

If, in the end, you realize your motivations have truly changed, and your long-term happiness won't be hindered by making a change, and it's not a matter of simply creating rewards for yourself along the way, then you shouldn't hesitate to move on. It's OK.*

Choose Your Own Disaster

The best stories come from near-disasters, but that doesn't mean they're much fun at the time. Once I started flying around the world every month, I also started making a series of dumb mistakes—double-booking myself on nonrefundable tickets, or showing up for flights I thought I'd reserved but hadn't. In some ways, I improved as I traveled more and more. I learned to pack a bag for two weeks in twenty minutes, and I rarely forgot something important. In other ways, however, I grew more careless. After I survived the first double-ticket debacle, it happened two more times.

In the Seychelles I made a huge error and, at the end of a four-night stay, misread the departure time for my return flight. Despite using the twenty-four-hour clock for years, for some reason I thought 20:00 was 10 p.m. instead of 8 p.m. I dutifully showed up more than two hours in advance, but as I walked into the check-in area, I noticed that no one else was there. Only a

---

* "When the facts change, I change my mind. When my information changes, I alter my conclusions." —commonly attributed to John Maynard Keynes.

few flights a day left from the tiny airport, and as I stood there trying to puzzle it out, I heard a big *whoosh!* overhead. *Hmmm, that's odd,* I thought. *Could that really be the only flight of the night taking off ten minutes early?* Indeed, it was.

The mishap was completely my mistake and I felt terrible. Yet as bad as it was, I also knew I could probably find an escape hatch. I immediately went into travel survivor mode and started flagging down people to ask questions. Were there any other flights? When was the next one? I was supposed to fly on Etihad Airways to Abu Dhabi, but what if I took Qatar Airways to Doha and connected? Was there a Skype connection I could use to start calling airlines? I went back to the hotel and arranged to stay another night. That evening, I made an initial plan to get out the following day, and in the morning I was able to confirm the flight with two quick calls.

I finally took off on that flight with no real harm done, feeling sheepish about making such a dumb mistake, but also glad that I'd kept my cool and managed to sort everything out. When misadventure strikes, you can panic or you can figure it out. One of these solutions is better than the other.

The DIY Support Team

If you've always felt like you don't fit in, one of the happiest experiences of your life will be discovering that there are others like you. Loneliness is part of many quests, but that doesn't mean you should *always* be lonely.

Some people I talked to felt strongly about not receiving help for their project. Others changed their minds as they went along. "Be open to contribution," wrote Sandi Wheaton, who

The DIY Support Team *(continued)*

traveled on Route 66 after being laid off at GM. "I used to try to do everything on my own, and then I realized this was a mistake. People want to help! So let them help."

Help can come in a variety of ways. Here are some examples of how people in this book were helped in their journeys.

- Gary Thorpe, who set out to produce the world's largest symphony, was assisted by the film team that was initially just documenting the project. After they stepped in, things moved a lot faster.

- Miranda Gibson, who spent more than four hundred days at the top of a eucalyptus tree in Tasmania, received hundreds of supportive emails and images from around the world on the one-year anniversary of her protest. Others sent donations or wrote letters to the Australian government on her behalf.

- Jia Jiang, who courted rejection through one hundred days of public experiments, relies on his wife as his best "idiot test." If he has a crazy idea that's worth pursuing, she cheers him on. If he has a crazy idea that's just crazy, she'll tell him that too.

- Howard Weaver, who led a team in taking down Alaska's leading newspaper, said that support came in all kinds of ways. In the early days, friends bought subscriptions to his planned paper, which didn't yet exist. Local bands played benefit concerts for free. Other supporters sold T-shirts door-to-door.

- Nancy Sathre-Vogel, matriarch of the "family on bikes" who cycled from Alaska to Argentina, said that there was hardly a day during their seventeen-thousand-mile journey when they weren't helped by someone. Whether it came in the form of bags of apples from strangers, offers of places to stay at guesthouses and hostels along the way, or emails from home, unexpected support became part of the routine.

"Visit Every Country" Timeline of Disasters, Pitfalls & Big Mistakes

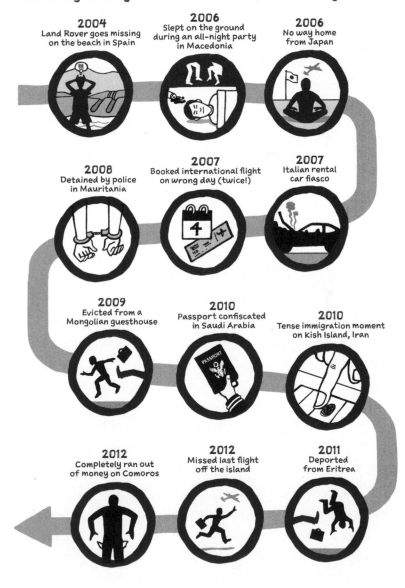

2004
Land Rover goes missing
on the beach in Spain

2006
Slept on the ground
during an all-night party
in Macedonia

2006
No way home
from Japan

2008
Detained by police
in Mauritania

2007
Booked international flight
on wrong day (twice!)

2007
Italian rental
car fiasco

2009
Evicted from a
Mongolian guesthouse

2010
Passport confiscated
in Saudi Arabia

2010
Tense immigration moment
on Kish Island, Iran

2012
Completely ran out
of money on Comoros

2012
Missed last flight
off the island

2011
Deported
from Eritrea

Regrets

Laura Dekker, the teenager who sailed the world's oceans on her own, said that she didn't regret anything. "There were moments where I was like, 'What the hell am I doing out here?'" she told a CNN reporter at the end of the voyage, "but I never wanted to stop. It's a dream, and I wanted to do it."

Another way to think of it is this: Regret is what you should fear the most. If something is going to keep you awake at night, let it be the fear of not following your dream. Be afraid of settling.

When Nate Damm set out to walk across America, he felt anxious and regretful almost right away. First came the practical problems: His feet hurt and he kept getting wet. These problems were easily solved—just keep walking, your feet will eventually get used to it, and buy the umbrella you should have packed in the first place. The deeper problems were the ones in his head. Before he left, Nate and his girlfriend broke up. Since he worked for her parents, the loss of a job soon followed. His cat and dog lived with her, so . . . he lost those too. It was like a bad country song: *Lost my girlfriend, lost my job, lost my dog.*

As Nate marched his way out of West Virginia, soaking wet from the rain and wincing at the blisters on his feet, he couldn't help wondering if he'd made the wrong decision. In the course of a single week, his life had completely flipped upside down.

His answer was different from Mark Boyle's. Nate overcame the doubt by looking forward. He thought about why he'd begun the walk in the first place. It wasn't for fame, it certainly wasn't for fortune, and he wasn't even trying to make a statement. He just had to do it—it was the crazy idea that wouldn't leave him alone, and the crazy idea demanded action.

Nate kept going and his mood brightened. Things back at home would never again be the same, but he realized there was an upside to all the change. The road opened up with possibilities.

❂

A continent away, Mark Boyle was almost instantly wrong when he set out from the docks of Dover, bound for India without a penny in his pocket. Failure came quickly as he realized his mission didn't translate on the shores of France, and soon he turned back to England feeling drained and embarrassed. The first few weeks at home were bittersweet. It was good to see family and friends, but Mark also carried a sense of guilt at having given up. "Don't worry about it, mate," a friend told him—but it wasn't that simple. The quest was important to Mark. He'd sacrificed in preparing for it, and it was hard to face the fact that he'd turned back.

Yet he still clung to his values. As more time passed, he began to see that the values themselves were what was truly important: embracing the "freeconomy" by choosing to live without money, and encouraging others to opt out of what he saw as excessive commercialism.

Hitchhiking to India was now off the list, but maybe there was another way he could live out those values.

Regrouping and reconsidering, Mark realized that he wasn't much of a world traveler. His interest in walking to India came from an attraction to Gandhi's lifestyle and philosophy, not from a desire to rough it across Afghanistan and other potentially hostile places. Instead of traveling, therefore, his new plan was simply to live without money.

He set up camp on an organic farm, trading three days' labor each week in return for a place to stay. He grew his own food, bathed in the river, and cycled to meetings with interested followers. Slowly he began speaking out again, owning up to his mistakes and positioning himself as a fellow learner instead of an expert who claimed to know it all.

His first quest had been strictly personal, but now Mark became an advocate for "life without money," using a solar-powered laptop to write articles for newspapers and blogs. He published a manifesto outlining his ideas. He created a forum with more than thirty thousand members, and he organized a "Freeconomy Festival" in Bristol that drew hundreds of curious attendees.

After the failure of his walking trip to India, the cashless Mark Boyle originally planned to pursue his new experiment for one year. More than two years later, he was still going strong. The new quest was the right one.

Remember

The right kind of misadventures—the ones that yield information—can produce confidence.

If you're going to worry about something, worry about the cost of *not* pursuing your dream.

Sometimes stopping is the right decision. When considering a shift, ask: Is my heart still in this?

III.
Destination

Chapter 15

Transformation

When you have completed 95 percent of your journey, you are only halfway there.
—JAPANESE PROVERB

Lesson: AS YOU MAKE PROGRESS TOWARD A
SMALL GOAL, THE BIGGER VISION EXPANDS.

In the end, all the clichés hold true: If you can't change the world, at least you can change yourself.

When I look back at what I wrote at the beginning of my journey, much of it seems naive or simplistic. I was taking on a challenge! I wanted to see the world! The world was . . . big. I didn't actually have much to say, it seems.

But this is how it usually happens. Part of it is the process of getting older, and part of it comes from the experience itself. In my case I realized that much of travel was about being open to different ways of life and changes outside my control. When I found myself getting frustrated, more often than not the problem was my own expectations.

As I was writing the first draft of this book, I took a trip to an island in Malaysia. I thought it would be a good place to visit while I worked on the manuscript, and it was. But when I mentioned where I was going to a few well-traveled friends, they were horrified. "That place is a tourist trap! Why would you go there?"

I went because I liked it . . . perhaps leading to another lesson: When it comes to travel, you should create your own itinerary and not have it be dictated by others.

Process vs. Achievement (To Nando's and Beyond)

People who pursue quests are often motivated by achievement, process, or simply a belief in daily adventure. How do these motivations affect what happens toward the end?

1. The achievement-motivated person wants to accomplish *something (scale the wall, rid the empire of invaders, and so forth).*

For some people, the motivator is a measurable challenge that will take a long time to complete. My brother Ken once sent me a link to a promotion from Nando's, a South African restaurant chain. I'd been introduced to Nando's while living in Africa several years earlier, and had also visited their restaurants in Dubai, Beirut, and Singapore. The email was entitled "Your next challenge!" When I clicked on the link, I saw what Ken meant: Nando's was offering a lifetime's worth of free meals to anyone who could prove they'd visited each of their restaurant locations in more than twenty countries.

For a moment, I felt oddly excited by the idea . . . before realizing how ridiculous it was. Would I really consider going all over the world in search of a lifetime pass at a fast-food restaurant where the average meal costs less than $10?* Yet here I

---

*As a vegetarian, I don't even eat peri-peri chicken—the featured menu item at Nando's. I do, however, recommend their veggie burgers.

was, thinking about the number of locations I'd already visited and kicking myself for not saving the receipts.

An achievement-motivated person will consider, if only briefly, visiting every location of a global restaurant chain. Everyone else will immediately dismiss the idea. Fortunately, most people are called to do something greater than seeking out french fries across the globe.

> *2. The process-motivated person wants to do something (collect or build in a step-by-step fashion, go on a long journey, and so forth).*

Isabelle Leibler, who trained an untrainable horse, says that she was almost entirely motivated by the process of training. The achievement (winning the national and North American dressage championships) was just a by-product. Every day it was all about completing a checklist, measuring progress, and making a plan for the next day.

Sasha Martin, who planned to cook a meal from every country for her young family, said that the steady process of "one country, one week" kept her going. There was a chart and a countdown. Without the clear sense of tackling the cooking project in stages, seeing countries get ticked off and planning ahead to the next one, she says she might have given up. Many other people I talked to also mentioned the importance of measurable progress. Count things down! Check them off! Be aware of your progress as you proceed down a path.

A Tale of Two Travelers

Nate Damm and Matt Krause both undertook walking quests, attempting to cross entire countries. Nate trekked across

America in seven and a half months, and Matt made it across Turkey in six. Yet when I asked them whether they focused more on process or achievement, their answers couldn't be more different. Here's Nate, who started in Maine and ended in San Francisco:

> I'm definitely not motivated by achievement. I just do what I like every day, and good things seem to happen as a result. I rarely thought about getting to San Francisco and completing the trek. In fact, I was upset when I actually did make it there, because then it was over and I had to go home for a while. The arrival at the ocean represented the completion of a big achievement, but it was really just another city. My experiences in a small town in Kansas, for example, were much more meaningful to me.

And here's Matt, who started on Turkey's western coast and ended 1,305 miles later at the Iranian border:

> Love the result, not the process. It sure helps if you enjoy the process, because you're going to have to spend a lot of time there before you see any results. But still, the process can kiss my ass. Throw processes under the bus if they aren't getting the desired result.

Which perspective is better? Perhaps the best way to think of it is that the two are inextricably intertwined. You can't achieve anything deeply satisfying without a drawn-out process leading up to it—and yet process demands a goal. You can't love one without at least appreciating the other.

Time Makes Changes

It's inevitable: Undertake a quest or any long, challenging project, and you won't come out of it the same. As I came to the end of my own mission, I talked with others who'd either finished what they started or were considerably under way. How were they changed through their quest? A few key themes emerged.

Change Number One: Independence and Confidence

Isabelle Leibler, who trained the untrainable horse, shared how the struggle had given her strength:

I definitely feel wiser. Before this quest, I was a mentally young athlete. I was fiery and dedicated and I wanted to give everything my all because somehow that would determine a win. However, following the quest, I realized that the only true strength you will ever need comes from you, and you alone. I became really independent and confident as a result of this quest, knowing that going forward your heart and mind are all you have when you're in the middle of an arena with ten thousand people watching. You have to embrace it, tighten it, and then let it all explode.

Nate Damm, who walked across America, experienced an entire personality change:

Before the walk, I was really quiet, shy, and uncomfortable in most social situations. The best thing that the walk did for me was make me confident that I could handle even the toughest of tests and scenarios, from knocking on the door of a stranger's house and asking if I could camp on their property to almost getting run over by big trucks. Every day had its challenges, and I'm actually very thankful for all of them.

Gabriel Wyner, an opera singer, began his language studies simply with the desire to improve his singing skills. As he mastered several tough languages in a short period of time, he shifted his focus:

The quest took over a great deal of my life. I set out to become a more expressive singer through languages, and ended with an obsession that is competing with my singing for attention and time. At least for the moment, languages are my life; I spend every day writing about them, learning them, and reading about them.

Change Number Two: Maturation

Rita J. King directs Science House, a global community and event space that helps businesses brainstorm ideas related to humans and technology. In an email from a trip to Italy, she provided a good example of how the process of pursuit can create a deeper perspective:

I have always been a playful, inquisitive person, focused on science and art, an avid learner, a passionate observer and participant in the human condition. But I am mature now. I listen much more. I feel comfortable letting things unfold even while I maintain a breakneck pace with my own work. My concepts of identity have become far more fluid.

In his early days of silence and walking, John Francis was a rebel. Part of not speaking to anyone and refusing all motorized transport was an act of rebellion. It was a peaceful protest, but John acknowledged being imbued with the spirit of "fighting the man" as he asserted his independence.

In one scene from his memoir, he became angry at a man who took his photo as he sat beside a gas station. The man's car was a state vehicle, and John worried that officials from the state of California were somehow going to exploit his protest for the state's benefit. He visited a lawyer friend who informed him of a public city council hearing held once a month in Sacramento. John went to the hearing—on foot, of course—and pleaded his case through a sign language interpreter. The comptroller running the meeting was kind, and assured John that nothing bad would happen with his photograph.

Later John realized what seemed obvious to everyone else: Maybe it's not that big of a deal that someone took a photo of him. The state of California may have its problems, but plotting to use John's image in a nefarious way is probably not one of them. Besides, from a practical standpoint, it didn't make sense to get upset every time someone wanted a photo. John was African American, with a scraggly beard and a large backpack he carried everywhere. He'd also begun carrying a banjo and playing it as he walked along the road. It's not every day that you meet someone who fits such a description, smiling but not speaking to anyone. There are going to be photos.

In the end, John made an even bigger change. He decided to start speaking again, and a few years later, he even began riding in cars. Here's how he explained the change:

After twenty-two years of walking, my decision not to use motorized vehicles had become a prison, and only I could set myself free. While I still continued my walking, I also decided to begin to fly and use motorized transportation to do other work. The lesson for me was to always revisit my decisions in the light of new knowledge and information. Don't be afraid to change.*

Change Number Three: Small Vision → Bigger Vision

Most of my early travels were solo excursions. It was just me and the world, and I didn't mind being alone. As I made progress toward the goal, though, I began to connect with more and more people. Readers would say hello in airports and coffee shops. I held meetups on every continent, where I learned more about the local culture than I would have with my nose stuck in a guidebook.

And then, just as I was nearing the end of the quest, I began to see that the next big adventure would be different. I'm not the first person to visit every country in the world, and I didn't plan on going to the moon, reaching the deepest part of the ocean, or anything else like that. (Feel free to take on these goals for yourself—someone should!)

I wasn't the greatest traveler in the world, and probably not the greatest anything. What I realized, though, was that I was making a shift from individually minded goals to group-minded goals. A big part of my next focus, and perhaps even a quest of its own, would be engaging more with the great people I met around the world and whom I regularly heard from online.

I wasn't the only person on a quest to find his perspective shifting. Many people talked about how their initial idea came

---

* This quote from John comes from a profile in the *Atlantic*. Other quotes come from his memoir *Planetwalker* or my email interviews with him.

to seem small as they matured and gained confidence. Sasha Martin, who set out to cook meals from around the world for her family in Oklahoma, saw her project quickly expand:

I expected the adventure to change our eating habits, but I didn't expect it to affect all other aspects of my life. My focus has shifted from our diets, which are now vastly improved, to sharing a message of peace through understanding at schools, dinners, and other major events. I am also writing a memoir about the experience and will build up to a big feast called "the Two-Hundred-Foot Table."

Tom Allen, who cycled from England to Iran, stopping along the way to fall in love, saw his initial quest of self-discovery become much more:

Instead of completing a single-minded lap of the planet and returning home victorious, as many others have done, I found myself reconnected with people by life on the road. I met and married my wife in Armenia, and launched a series of storytelling projects that has grown to inspire others. And alongside all of this I continue traveling on my original quest. Having pushed the limits of bicycle travel, from roadless Outer Mongolia to the Arctic in winter to crossing the Sahara and Afar deserts, I want to see how much further it can go.

Allie Turner, who set out to visit every basilica in the United States with her boyfriend Jason, adopted a more active approach to life:

It's given us a greater awareness and appreciation for the little things. We've come to recognize that there is a large amount of magnificent architecture and history waiting for us, most of it in small-town America where many of the basilicas reside. We spend more time looking for adventure on the way to where we're going, rather than waiting for adventures to come to us, or making elaborate plans to visit some of the more common cities to look for adventure.

If You Don't Like the Menu, Leave the Restaurant

Don't settle: Don't finish bad books. If you don't like the menu, leave the restaurant. If you're not on the right path, get off it. —Chris Brogan

A friend of mine gave notice from her job as an associate professor at a small private university. She taught only the classes she wanted, and only in the way she wanted. The administration supported her with academic freedom. She had a good salary and full benefits, with lots of breaks and every summer off to pursue other projects.

Why leave? "Because it was time," she said. Just because it was a good job didn't mean that she had to do it forever. Everything has a season.

Some of our mutual friends didn't understand why she was closing the door on an opportunity that had served her well. According to her, though, she had to leave to find something new. The right time to leave is when you're ready, not just when someone else makes the decision for you.

Do *all* good things come to an end? That's a debate for another book. But when a good thing reaches its natural end, don't drag it out. If you don't like the menu, leave the restaurant.

Change Number Four: Empowerment

When I talk with people about self-employment, I often tell the story of how excited I was to earn $1.26 one day in Belgium many years ago. I was passing through town for a couple of days and had conducted an online experiment with some new ads. I set up a very small test and went out for the day, traveling to Luxembourg and back. When I returned in the evening I saw that the test was successful: I'd made $1.26 in net income. It may not sound like a gold rush, but I was excited because I knew it represented something greater. If that small test worked, the odds were promising that it would work on a larger scale. It was the best dollar I'd ever made.

I felt something similar when I entered the final stretch of thirty countries. I still had some big challenges ahead, including a number of destinations that had eluded me for years, but I had little doubt that I could see it through. *I can take on the world,* I thought. *There's nothing I can't do.*

If you can't wrap your head around going everywhere, or producing a symphony with hundreds of performers, or undertaking any of the other quests I've described so far, it's important to remember that dreams tend to grow as you pursue them.

As you gain confidence, "I can do this!" becomes "What else can I do?"

Over and over again, the people I talked to said that their quest had inspired an even greater vision for their next project. Steve Kamb, who redesigned his life to follow the pattern of a video game, said that he'd never felt stronger or more powerful.

Until I was twenty-six I remained stuck on the couch, playing games in which my character would level up in order to explore foreign lands that were unsafe or inaccessible at a lower level. But now I'm doing that in real life! I'm the character who is growing in strength and wisdom.

Steve's strength and wisdom came through getting off the couch and making a game of his life—with much higher stakes than he'd found in front of the TV or computer monitor. He continued to level up, taking on greater challenges and feeling firmly in control of his future.

Remember

Pursuing a quest can boost your confidence and establish your independence.

Those who pursue quests find themselves focusing more and expanding their vision as they go along.

"I'm glad I did it" was the most common statement from people who'd completed a quest.

Dispatch

COMMUNITY

Every traveler has at least one story of unexpected hospitality or generosity that exceeded all assumptions. As I roamed the world, I collected a legion of these lessons in kindness. For every taxi driver who tried to rip me off, there was another who undercharged. Getting lost everywhere I went, yet always finding my way back—in some ways it was a testament to independence, but in others it spoke to the inherent good nature of people everywhere. These good Samaritans would break off from whatever they were doing to point the way to the main road, or sometimes even bring me back to my guesthouse with a smile. Stubborn as I was about doing things my own way, I came to rely on the kindness of strangers on every continent.

In Croatia I stayed with a host family who translated the local reality TV shows for my benefit. In Kuwait I was hosted by Haider Al-Mosawi, a local blogger who'd written me in advance to say he was a "Kuwaiti nonconformist" and wanted to show me around.

Even in places with a reputation for danger or hostility, I was almost always treated as a welcome guest. In Somaliland, the airport was three hours by bumpy road from the main city. Despite my protests, I was given the seat of honor in the crowded minibus, right up front with the driver. In Libya, just before the country fell into the revolution that toppled Muammar Gaddafi, my hosts carefully led me around Tripoli, pointing out Islamic architecture and making guarded comments about the dictatorship that held most of the country in its grip. When we stopped for coffee, they refused to let me pay.

In the Comoros, a small island nation off the coast of southern Africa, I found myself completely out of cash. I'd made numerous mistakes in letting such a thing happen, from underestimating the cost of the visa I had to purchase upon arrival to overestimating the odds of ATMs being available. Simply put, I didn't have enough money, so the immigration officer held on to my passport. She agreed I could visit the country and stay two nights, but to reclaim my passport and get off the island, I'd need to pay up. On the morning of departure I still didn't have the money, and I was stressed.

I tried everything I could think of, including a mad dash across the island to visit the only working ATM—which didn't work.

In the end I was saved, not by my own ingenuity but by the providential appearance of a stranger who loaned me money. In exchange for his trust I gave him all the funds I had left (about $30 composed of several different currencies), a copy of a book I'd written ("This is me!"), and a promise to somehow pay him back. He gave me $60 in local currency, reclaimed my passport, and waved me off.

❂

Over and over throughout the journey, I learned and relearned an important lesson of humanity. When I'd first gone abroad, originally on a summer trip to China, I returned with a perspective typical of the bedazzled novice traveler: "*People everywhere are the same!*"

But as I learned with more experience, that wasn't the case at all. Sure, the wide swath of humanity has a few things in common: No matter where you go, most parents love their children, and most people want to be happy in their own way. Otherwise, though, it shouldn't be surprising that different cultures produce widely different practices and belief structures—and it's this very fact that makes travel and exploration so intoxicating. Touring the Buddhist temples of Bhutan, a small Asian nation that welcomes far fewer tourists than its neighbors India and Nepal . . . visiting the Great Mosque at sunset in the old city of Damascus . . . hopping an overnight train to Tbilisi, Georgia, and talking with a fellow traveler from another foreign land—instead of evaluating how they stacked up against my own preconceptions and preferences, I came to appreciate the differences on their own merit.

As I approached the end of my quest, I tried to pay more attention to my surroundings. Though having a goal was important—I believed in the list!—the quest was never about conquering an arbitrary grouping of countries. It was about challenging myself to pursue a big goal, and allowing myself to change as I went along.

Chapter 16

Homecomings

Home is where you go when you run out of homes.

— JOHN LE CARRÉ

Lesson: MAKE A PLAN FOR THE NEXT STEP.

In the anthology *Once Upon a Galaxy,* science fiction author Josepha Sherman chronicles the long history of ancient stories and shows how they serve as models for modern-day fables. As we've seen in this book, very different quests tend to have a number of things in common. In the ancient stories there is often a search for a mythical object (a sacred necklace, a holy grail), or a need to reclaim something that has been stolen. A "wise old man" figure who foresees tests and trials for the brave adventurer often offers guidance. The hero is joined by friends and allies, some of whom may have their own agendas.*

Other figures creep up again and again in different stories. Babies destined for greatness are rescued from small boats or boxes (Moses, Superman). The world of nature has its share of mythical creatures (eagles, horses, spiders). Rings are often objects of power and magic. ("One ring to rule them all.")

---

*Obi-Wan Kenobi: "Things are changing. And sometimes the line between friend and foe is blurred. Now more than ever."

But then something unusual happens—and it's not the "big surprise" we've come to expect. In story after story, we hear of great adventures. And then, all of a sudden, the stories end with a fizzle, grinding to a halt without much explanation.

The classic story of Jason and the Argonauts is typical. Jason is born a prince, but is then snatched away in the middle of the night as a baby. He grows up in a foreign land, unaware of his birthright. Fortunately, his tutor is a wise-old-man figure who raises him right, giving him the news of his true identity once he reaches adulthood. Jason then sets out to reclaim his throne, confronting the king who'd pushed aside Jason's father.

The king is as wise as Jason is ambitious, so in a classic old-school stalling tactic, he sends Jason away on a dangerous quest. "Go and recapture the Golden Fleece!" he orders, not mentioning the part about the monster responsible for guarding the treasure, which conveniently *never sleeps.*

The evidence will show that Jason is especially brave or foolhardy, depending on your view of monsters guarding fleeces. He dutifully gathers a team of heroes, builds the strongest ship that has ever sailed the treacherous Mediterranean waters, and sets out in search of the fleece.

But then! Trouble strikes along the path. The adventurers are waylaid time and again. On an island filled with murderous women they're nearly entrapped, but they get away in the nick of time. On another island the inhabitants are being tormented by giants, and Jason's crew are the only ones who can fend them off. A third stop brings winged creatures that attack from the sky. Then there are the magical rocks that smash together whenever a ship tries to pass through, and . . . on and on.

In this manner Jason and the Argonauts sail and struggle through a dozen years of trial and tribulation. Finally, they reach their destination. *This is it!* But even then they're tested. There's a herd of fire-breathing bulls that have to be yoked, a set of dragon's teeth that must be obtained, and a bunch of warriors that spring from the ground that must be defeated. With some help from a new girlfriend, Jason finally completes all the necessary tasks. Escaping in the dead of night with the fleece and the girlfriend, Jason and his fellow Argonauts set sail for home. They've done it!

But then what? What happens after all this effort? What happened to the throne that Jason was looking to reclaim?

Josepha Sherman tells the story as it has been recorded in history, with different variations but the same common ending: "Many more adventures awaited Jason. While some of those adventures were heroic, others were tragic. But the future was the future."

That's it? "The future was the future?"

Indeed, that's all we get.

It's easy to feel let down after so much effort . . . but that's how it works. Quests don't always tie up well.

The World Is Saved . . . Somehow

This pattern is not confined to stories of old. Video games and movies often exhibit the same abrupt endings. For research purposes in my early twenties, I devoted hundreds of hours to the study of video games. Much of the research was spent camped out with friends in my living room, dutifully shooting on-screen characters in the head with a sniper rifle, but many other hours were spent in solitary study. With only a large supply of Diet Coke and the occasional Krispy Kreme donut for nourishment,* I plodded through dungeons and sped across entire galaxies seeking to rescue a civilization or find my character's original self.

Even for research purposes, you don't invest twenty to thirty hours in a game that sucks. The best games keep users challenged and entertained through a long series of levels, quests, and animation scenes that move the story forward.

But you know what? Even the best games often have bad endings. My friends and I would often make a marathon effort to complete the latest game, and while the journey was enthralling, the ending was a letdown. Sometimes I'd call my brother Ken after completing a game he'd already beaten. "That was awesome!" we'd both say. "But the ending"—we agreed— "was weird."

It was as if, after creating a great story and bringing the character through trials and tribulations, the game's designers had suddenly thrown up their hands in resignation. "We don't know what happens in the end! Our job was to keep the story going!" they seemed to be saying.

Is this principle at work in modern-day quests as well? Indeed—sometimes it is.

"What's It Like?"

Over seven long days in 2009, and then again in 2010 and 2012, Meghan Hicks ran the Marathon des Sables, a 150-mile race in the Sahara Desert. Every year at least eight hundred runners descend on Morocco for this race, and as Meghan

---

* It's important to eat well when saving the world.

puts it, everyone who attempts it is a little strange—but some are stranger than others.

Meghan was an experienced runner who knew what she was getting into. She was the kind of runner whose biggest problem was overtraining. She loved being on the trails of her native Utah and had constructed a lifestyle that allowed her to be outside as often as possible. To maintain her intense training schedule in the winter months, she actually created a makeshift sauna in her house. The sauna effect was achieved by first installing a heater in the bathroom then turning on the hot water in the shower. She squeezed a stationary bike between the sink and toilet for her workouts.

Despite all of Meghan's training for the 2012 event, and despite having done it before, the moment of setting out that first morning in the Sahara was a shock to her senses. Every day for the next week Meghan struggled through the sand, dreaming of the dehydrated green beans that would await her at day's end. (When you're malnourished and dehydrated, running dozens of miles through the desert, apparently they're a great snack.)

As tough as it was, Meghan eventually acclimated to the routine of mile after mile in the sand, and surged to the head of the pack. She would have found a kindred spirit in Nate Damm, who said that walking across America was "pretty simple" because all he had to do was put one foot in front of the other. In Meghan's case, she had to do that in 100°F heat in the middle of the desert. She finished her 2012 race in fifth place among women and placed forty-seventh overall. It was a huge victory.

And then she came home. Everyone asked the big question, "What was it like?"

Some really wanted to know, but others were just being polite. Here's what Meghan had to say:

They ask a complex question, but seek a one-sentence answer. It's akin to inquiring, "In seven words or less, describe your relationship with God." So you say, "The race was wonderful" and "I loved it" and "It's an experience I hope I don't forget." These statements are true but they toss a fuzzy, feel-good blanket over the whole Sahara Desert. There is no short answer for that question.

When you've given everything you have in pursuit of something great, it's hard to toss off a few quick sentences on "what it's like."

☯

Coming home from Norway, I felt a lot like Meghan. "What's it like to visit every country in the world?" I was asked.

People have the expectation that you're now very wise, that you've somehow acquired the knowledge of a thousand civilizations merely by passing through as a sojourner. They expect you to return with a sense of altered perspective and something profound to share.

Conquering planet Earth as a modern explorer *is* amazing. But coming to the end of such a quest is also complicated.

"Going to every country in the world" had been my identity for a long time. Even as I pursued other goals, the quest served as an important anchor. As I evaluated upcoming plans at the end of the year, I always considered them against the need to visit a dozen or more new countries. I knew I'd still be traveling after the quest was complete, but not with the same imperative. I was free to choose . . . and freedom seemed overwhelming.

Like Meghan Hicks in her post-Sahara experience, I had to deal with two big challenges: the public aspect of it and the inner aspect. For the public aspect, I eventually stumbled on a clear answer: Don't try to explain everything, but do tell a few good stories. For the private aspect, I learned to reflect—and also to consider the future.

Part One: Focus on the Stories.

After my journey was over, I went on a number of radio shows where the host inevitably began with at least one false or misleading statement. "Chris has been to more than three hundred countries!" (Uh, there aren't that many.) "Chris is the first person in the world to ever do this!" (Not true.) "Chris is only twenty-five years old!" (I wish.)

Then, after a long lead-up to gain the audience's rapt attention, the questioning would begin. "So what was it like, Chris?"

Yeah . . . what *was* it like? No pressure.

Like Meghan, I didn't know how to answer. "It was amazing," I said, knowing how trite it sounded. "It was a dream come true" . . . which it was, but that sounded dumb, too.

I usually fumbled along for a while before finding an answer. During one of the shows, an experienced interviewer reminded me that I didn't have to sum up 193 countries and ten years of travel in a few sentences. "Just tell us a story or two," he said.

That's right—those stories. I remember now. Remember just a few months ago, I told myself, *when you spent the night on the floor of the Dakar airport? The situation was comically awful, but you got through it and made it to the final country.*

Remember walking on the beach at midnight in Sri Lanka, the one hundredth country?

Remember that guy in Comoros who rescued me, loaning money to a stranger?

Remember those sunsets . . . those moments of wonder . . . the challenge, the process, the waiting? That's right—that's what it was about. When in doubt, come back to the stories.

Part Two: Process and Reflect.

Miranda Gibson had lived in a tree for more than a year. When she left, she was overwhelmed. She wrote on her blog:

> *Over the past few weeks I've tried many times to write to let you know what this has been like—getting down, adjusting to the world on the ground. But every time I sit down to write I don't know what to say. It is so overwhelming—everything that has taken place and all I have thought and felt these past few months. It felt impossible to know where to start. Today I have told you the story of my feet touching the ground, but now that I've started writing there are so many more stories that want to come tumbling out: of the fire, my last day in the tree, my first day in a house!*

Around the same time, Alicia Ostarello went home to California after visiting forty-eight of the fifty states on her "adventures in dating" tour. She still had to fly to Hawaii and Alaska, but she was nearly at the end. For the first time in months, she didn't have a goal for the next day. Not only that,

248 • The Happiness of Pursuit

but having given up her apartment to pursue the cross-country project, she no longer had a place to live. She had friends with couches and a bed at her parents' home thirty miles away, but those solutions felt like a step backward. She'd come all this way! She'd learned so much! And now she sat in her car—oddly the most familiar environment to her after months of driving—and tried not to cry.

In the classic children's book *The Phantom Tollbooth,* the main character Milo and his helpful friends are waylaid by a tall, thin man who assigns them mundane, tedious tasks. Being an agreeable sort, Milo acquiesces, only to discover that the tall man is actually the devil, who delights in pulling people off their chosen paths.

Alicia thought of this story after she jumped into a new job as a production assistant in the events industry, a challenging role that required ten-hour days and a lot of focus. It was a great job for someone with abundant energy to invest in a new career, but not ideal for someone coming off an extended trip around the country in search of herself. She felt like Milo. She'd been diverted, and the busy days at work prevented her from processing the intense experience she'd just been through. The whole experience felt weird and incomplete.

Lesson: Don't forget to debrief. You may need another goal at some point, but be careful to process before jumping back into the grind.

Part Three: Find the Next Quest!

If a quest or adventure has kept you enthralled for years, but has now come to an end in a blaze of glory (or even a blaze of calm), sooner or later you'll need a new project. As Alicia learned, you might not want to jump into something else right away, but you also shouldn't wait too long.

Scott Young devoted a full year to mastering the four-year MIT computer science curriculum. When he finished, he worked on other projects for a while, but found he missed the daily aspect of making progress toward a big goal. Even though his routine contained little variation during the year of studying, he found it challenging and stimulating. He decided to try a similar approach with something else: This time, he'd spend a year learning several languages. As a twist (there's always a twist) he wouldn't speak English *at all* during the year. Before he could talk himself out of this big new goal, he boarded a flight for Valencia despite not speaking Spanish. When he disembarked he would speak *only* Spanish and any other language besides English. An entire year not speaking your native language—is that a quest? It certainly sounds like a big challenge.

Woe Is Me, All Is Lost, etc.

In an early scene from *The Shawshank Redemption*, Brooks Hatlen is released from prison after being locked up for fifty years. He then hangs himself, unable to cope with life on the outside.

Writing more than 160 years ago, John Stuart Mill reflected on the fleeting sense of happiness.

> *"Suppose that all your objects in life were realized; that all the changes in institutions and opinions which you are looking forward to, could be completely effected at this very instant: would this be a great joy and happiness to you?" And an irrepressible self-consciousness distinctly an-*

swered, "No!" At this my heart sank within me: the whole
foundation on which my life was constructed fell down.
All my happiness was to have been found in the continual
pursuit of this end. The end had ceased to charm, and
how could there ever again be any interest in the means?
I seemed to have nothing left to live for.

Well, that sounds a bit depressing. Nothing left to live for?
Hanging yourself after being released from prison?

Maybe these aren't the final answers, or at least they
shouldn't be.

Howard Weaver rose from failed attempts at tailing mobsters
and, after a long drinking session, throwing rocks at the *An-*
chorage Times building to become a lead protagonist in an epic
battle to take down the establishment and alter the balance of
political conversation in Alaska. The early years were rough,
bringing two divorces and a struggle with alcohol.

By the time he took control of the editor's office at the
Daily News, the *Times'* competition, he'd quit drinking, settled
down with a longtime partner, and focused steadfastly on taking down the enemy. The final stage of the battle would last a
dozen years, but as Howard saw it, the truth finally won out.
When the *Times* shuttered its doors in 1992, the long-hoped-
for victory had been secured.

Waiting around the corner for Howard, though, was an
even bigger question than those he'd faced during the spir-
ited newspaper wars: What's next? "Now I was tired and dis-
oriented," he wrote. "Though we'd won what I thought was

lasting security for the *Daily News* and its fiercely independent journalism, the absence of the *Times* was oddly haunting . . . . A large part of how I'd defined myself simply was no longer there."

This wasn't just an existential crisis; Howard really didn't know what to do next. He asked for a sabbatical and went to England. He earned a master's degree, planning to return to the helm, but when he returned to Alaska after the year's leave he saw that things were different. A new publisher was in charge, with vastly different ideas. Right from the beginning, the new publisher and Howard found themselves at odds, disagreeing on editorial positions and even the daily reporting style that had been established through precedent over many years.

Finally Howard realized that the situation wasn't going to change anytime soon. He had enough clout to continue to fight the daily battle over editorials, but was worn out from fighting the bigger war. A native son who'd lived in Alaska for almost all of his life, he reluctantly moved to California to take on a new job. Once he'd won the war against the *Times,* things were never quite the same. Even the departure from the *Daily News* didn't go well, when the publisher declined to hire his close friend and chosen successor. The paper's editorial voice continued to shift against Howard's hard-fought philosophy, and in the end he adopted a mixed sense of resignation and regret as he moved on to other work.*

---

* In his memoir, Howard quotes H. G. Wells: "It is the universal weakness of mankind that what we are given to administer, we presently imagine we own."

But Where Is Home, Actually?

After traveling the world for eight years, Benny Lewis calls himself a "humanist," meaning that he loves people and values their worth more than anything else. Benny grew up in Ireland, a predominately Catholic country, and after university gradually expanded his worldview by traveling.

I've hung out with Benny on three continents so far, beginning at a meetup in Thailand and continuing to a tour together in Scandinavia. Recently, when we met in a coffee shop in Oregon, he told me about his conversion to humanism. It wasn't a rebellion against his faith, he said, it was just a result of gaining a general awareness of the rest of the world.

We talked about how we'd each adopted habits of different cultures as we moved from place to place. I became a vegetarian right before traveling to India for the first time, and the food of South Asia soon became my favorite. Though I still liked America and enjoyed living there much of the time, I felt more like a world citizen. The distinguishing marks of a passport didn't determine my identity; my experiences and values did.

The more you experience something outside of what you've known, the more open-minded you become . . . but this worldview can also be somewhat alienating, especially to people at home. Another friend, Shannon O'Donnell, left home at the age of twenty-four on a voyage of self-discovery. She originally set out for Los Angeles, as far away from her home in Florida as she could initially imagine. An acquaintance who'd spent several months in India inspired her to look further, and she prepared to go overseas.

Shannon's short-term goal was to spend a year abroad, a journey that was personally enriching but not terribly unusual.

She backpacked around Australia and Southeast Asia, visiting almost ten countries, and then went on to visit several more in Europe. "The path I had been on wasn't working," she said later, "so I thought a radical change of pace would give me a way to live a more purposeful life. I wanted to learn from the people and places I encountered on my travels."

She described the year abroad as "boot-camp to life," and shared how she completed a ten-day meditation course in Nepal despite having little previous experience with the practice. The course was challenging, both mentally and physically, and she had little desire to continue after the end—but even though intensive mediation wasn't for her, she gained an appreciation for how others find happiness.

Shannon has often been prone to illness, and in Laos she became very ill with dysentery. In a low moment, feeling like she might not even make it through the night, she made a bargain with the universe: *If I get better, I'll trade my recovery for a more traditional life. I'll get on a plane and pursue the things that most people want: a home, a spouse, and children.*

Except the things that most people wanted weren't what *she* wanted, at least not right away. Shannon made it through the long night, and as she recovered she looked back on the bargain and realized how foolish it was: "At that moment I blamed the very idea of my aimless wandering for my illness, but as I healed I realized that the illness was a setback, not a sign that I was on the wrong path."

The original journey of one year has now lasted more than five, and for much of the time she has been accompanied by her eleven-year-old niece, who joined her in Asia for an immersion experience like no other.

254 • The Happiness of Pursuit

The Real World Is What You Make It

Perhaps the biggest adjustment to life at "home," wherever home may be, is understanding that you're different from when you started. You've gained experience and seen things that others haven't. To quote the words of Steve Kamb, who used the analogy of a video game with me in describing his quest, you've "leveled up." In the same way that the first level of a game can become boring and repetitive, once you've leveled up, you may not be able to go back to the same habits and routine.

Several people I spoke with for this book described how, after they'd finished their quests, they'd heard a certain phrase uttered by their friends and family. The phrase was "real life" or "the real world," and the words were sometimes delivered callously. "Guess you'll have to get back to real life now" was one way of putting it. "That would never work in the real world" was another. At other times phrases like these were invoked more innocently, perhaps by someone who just couldn't relate to what had happened during the quest.

Tom Allen said that people who applied this kind of logic had it exactly backward. "Life on the road *was* the real world," he reflected. "Back in England, it was modern society that seemed to be a place of isolation and abstractions."

How do you go back? In many ways, you don't. You can't.

In Tom's case, he was also disappointed that at least some of the quest had been tainted by its own institutionalization. What started as an adventure in self-discovery had become a global endeavor, complete with sponsors who expected reports and media outlets that were eager to interview him. He finally had to unwind what he created and "deinstitutionalize the beast," focusing once again on the no-strings-attached journey he'd longed for from the beginning.

Recovery

To climb out of a post-quest funk, you start by realizing that the real world is what you make of it. You've grown, you've changed, and you can't go back. You're not the same, so don't expect everyone else to be the same either.

Next, you start again. You need a new quest and a new mission.

In the foothills of central California, a flag flies above a small ranch home. The home belongs to Howard Weaver, the newspaper editor who challenged a giant and won. The flag is the former property of the *Anchorage Times*. Is it petty to fly the flag of your defeated rival? Some might say so . . . but Howard treasures the flag as a reminder of his principled fight for truth and justice in his native Alaska.

In a historic San Francisco apartment building a couple hours north of Howard's ranch, Alicia Ostarello settled back into life as a copywriter. She kept only one memento from her journey: a postcard from South Dakota, which she attached to the mirror in her room. She'd moved on to other things, regrouping from the emotional experience of ending a big project—but every once in a while, she'd see the postcard and would remember driving mile after mile throughout the country, counting down the states and meeting new people at every stop.

Alicia and Howard both turned out OK.

Meanwhile, Meghan Hicks finished her fourth Marathon des Sables race and started planning for the next. She continued to train every day.

Remember

Sometimes quests don't tie up well. Sometimes it's hard at the end.

If it's hard to explain the totality of a quest, focus on a few stories.

The real world is what you make of it. After completing a quest, the next steps are up to you.

Chapter 17

Finale

It is always important to know when something has reached its end. Closing circles, shutting doors, finishing chapters, it doesn't matter what we call it; what matters is to leave in the past those moments in life that are over. —PAULO COELHO

Lesson: THE END IS THE BEGINNING.

How did it feel when Nate Damm arrived at the Pacific Ocean after walking across America? It was amazing, of course. All that surf in the San Francisco Bay, all those people welcoming him in person and sending congratulations online. But he was always a quiet guy, and this sense of arrival was bittersweet. The quest had given him hope, identity, and a recurring task: Every day, he simply had to get up and walk. Once his feet touched the cold water of the bay, he no longer had to do that.

In one of our conversations, he even used the word *annoyed* when describing the end—as if he was distressed that the quest that had consumed his life the past seven months was now over.

How did it feel when Gary Thorpe, the Australian classical music enthusiast, saw the production of the Gothic Symphony brought to life? Reflecting on the performance immediately afterward, he was effusive. "It's an imperishable monument, like the Pyramids or Stonehenge," he said. "The whole thing was breathtaking. The audience response was just as I'd hoped for all that time."

He was thrilled it had happened and couldn't be happier.

I thought of Nate and Gary when I touched down in Oslo, Norway, after a short flight from London Heathrow. I'm not sure it was a Pyramid-worthy moment. There was no two-hundred-member string section waiting to perform. Instead, the immigration clerk held my passport to the scanner and asked a couple of questions without looking at me. "Why have you come to Norway?"

I decided it would be best to omit the long story, so I told a short and truthful one: "I've always wanted to come."

❂

After a few mishaps in the final few countries, everything had gone well with getting to Guinea Bissau and Kiribati, the penultimate stops. In fact, I began my visit to Kiribati on New Year's Day, a full three months in advance of the final country visit in Norway. It was perhaps fitting that I ended up stranded on Kiribati when the twice-weekly flight to Fiji encountered mechanical issues and had to turn around, leaving me and the six other passengers stuck in the classic "no way off the island" scenario.

Kiribati doesn't rate high on most "must-see" travel lists, and I was eager to get back to Fiji and eventually homeward. I reminded myself of the ultimate travel skill (above all, a traveler must learn to wait) and reflected that this would be the very last time I was stranded, at least on this particular ten-year journey. Eventually the plane was fixed and we hopped on board for the three-hour flight. Just like that, it was done. Only one country to go!

Over the next couple of months I thought about how the adventure was almost complete. All I had to do was go to Norway, which presumably wouldn't be difficult. I thought of the line from Ithaca: "To arrive there is your ultimate goal, but do not hurry." I didn't hurry, and when the time came to board the flight for Heathrow and then the short connection to Oslo, I felt settled.

Every quest has an end. This story's ending arrived when I completed the immigration process and walked out to the airport train that would soon depart for the city. Or perhaps it ended as I went on a forty-eight-hour "Norway in a Nutshell" tour with my family and a few close friends. Maybe it ended the day after that, when nearly two hundred additional people arrived for an "End of the World" celebration we held for anyone who wanted to come.

The party was a good demonstration of how my life and the quest itself had evolved over the years. Whereas I began on my own, traipsing around as a solo traveler on an independent journey, I ended surrounded by good friends and other interesting people. Readers from more than twenty countries showed up. One guy had hitchhiked from Portugal on his own three-week journey of adventure, timing his arrival in Norway to enter our End of the World party with his backpack still on. Some people had specifically come to congratulate me, and the thought that they'd cross borders and buy plane tickets just for that was humbling.

But fortunately, it wasn't all about me. By now the adventure had grown to be about other people as well, and many of those in attendance were busy following dreams of their own and making connections with one another.

❂

After the end of the world in Norway I went to Hong Kong, winding down another round-the-world ticket on the long way back to my home in Portland. When the Cathay Pacific jet touched down and I walked through the terminal, I had all the time in the world. My ticket was fully flexible—I could go on to Bangkok the next day as scheduled, or I could stay in Hong Kong as long as I liked.

I cleared immigration, took the train to the city, and went looking for my hotel. Somehow I became lost. The rain was coming down as I took another wrong turn, schlepping my bags and looking in vain for a taxi. I was mad at myself for getting lost yet again, yet I appreciated the headline: "Man Visits Every Country; Can't Find Hotel He's Been to a Dozen Times." Typical.

I found the hotel eventually, as I always do. The next morning I stepped outside and wandered down Nathan Road, a place I'd come to know well since my very first trip to Hong Kong many years ago. That time I rode the bus in from the airport, stopping outside Cameron Road and a series of cheap hotels that were perched high above the city in residential buildings.

I stopped to look up at the Star Guest House, where I'd stayed for three nights on a trip long ago. I remember falling asleep at two p.m. and not waking up until after dark—one of the first times I made that mistake, but it turned out just fine since I spent much of the night wandering the streets. On a warm April day seven years later, Kowloon was buzzing with vendors offering fried insects and Portuguese egg tarts.

I'd made it to the end of the world, but Hong Kong was the same. Everyone else was going about their business, thinking their own thoughts and living their own life. In the city's financial sector, men and women in suits were hurrying out for a quick lunch before returning to their desks.

The next day I went to Bangkok and experienced similar flashbacks from my early years of traveling in Thailand. A familiar montage presented itself: the monks on the subway, the bustle of street traffic, and the narrow alleyways that connected much of the city.

Finally, I headed back to Portland via the madhouse of LAX airport. One more homecoming! Except there was nowhere else to go this time. There was no visa application to send to the embassy of South Sudan, no more plane tickets to be purchased on Air Moldova. My journey was complete.

❂

Hundreds of pages earlier, I said that this book wasn't just a study of what *other* people have done. The core message is that a quest can bring purpose and meaning to *your* life, too.

Why pursue a quest? Because each of us in our lives is writing our own story, and we only have one chance to get it right. Consider the words of Alicia Ostarello, who recovered from ending a relationship to taking on a dating mission that was simultaneously uncomfortable and enriching. Here's what she said when the quest was over: "This is my story. No one can take it from me. And that is what has made everything entirely worth it."

❂

At age sixty-eight, Phoebe Snetsinger had slowed her manic travel pace from years past, but she continued to undertake expeditions. The next stop on her itinerary was Madagascar, a country she was visiting for the fourth time. On the previous trips she'd seen the vast majority of local bird species, so this was a "cleanup trip" in pursuit of approximately twenty species that remained elusive. Seventeen years had elapsed since her "fatal" diagnosis, and while she was frailer than before, she scurried over trails despite having sprained an ankle. She also struggled with numerous other ailments due to advancing age, yet her notes from the trip are full of detailed descriptions of new birds she'd seen, as well as various tasks she needed to complete for upcoming trips.

Early on the morning of November 23, 1999, Phoebe and the rest of the group were traveling in a van toward another nature reserve. Phoebe lay down on the seats to nap. At some point, the driver fell asleep as well, or otherwise lost concentration. Traveling at full speed, the van scraped a concrete post and then tipped over on its side. The other passengers had minor injuries and were shaken up, but Phoebe took the brunt of the impact when the van tipped over. She died instantly.

Unbalanced as it may have been, the second half of Phoebe's life was spent in the way she intended. Like many others who pursue quests and big adventures, she'd learned to think differently about risk. As she wrote in her memoir: "It has

become ever more clear to me that if I had spent my life avoiding any and all potential risks, I would have missed doing most of the things that have comprised the best years of my life."

"The game never really ends," she continued in the last page of her memoir before the final trip to Africa. "It's simply a matter of perspective. There's always, as long as one lives, some new place to go, some exciting new thing to find." Yet for Phoebe, her quest met its end in Madagascar. She'd devoted nearly two decades to seeing more birds than anyone in history, she'd achieved her goal of breaking the world record, and she would have kept going if she could.

Dear Reader,

Thanks for joining me on the mini-quest of reading this book. If you enjoyed the journey, I'd love for you to share your story with our community at FindtheQuest.com. You can also write to me by visiting ChrisGuillebeau.com.

I hope to see you on the road somewhere.

Chris Guillebeau
#FindtheQuest

Appendix 1

Lessons from the Journey

From my own 193-country journey to the stories of many other people who were kindly willing to share, I've tried to extract and convey the lessons of modern-day quests. The experiences of fifty people pursuing big goals varies immensely, but a number of lessons are close to universal:

Unhappiness can lead to new beginnings. If you're not happy with your life, or even if you feel a faint stirring to do something different, pay attention to the dissatisfaction. Ask yourself "What if" questions. What if I actually pursued that dream or idea? What if I made that big change? Discontent can be a source of growth and inspiration.

Adventure is for everyone. You can have the life you want no matter who you are. There's a quest waiting for you to find, claim, or create.

Everyone has a calling. Follow *your* passion. Pay attention to the things that excite you and the things that bother you. Remember Jiro Ono, the sushi chef from Tokyo who talked about feeling victorious over a particularly nice tuna, and remember Miranda Gibson, who lived in the treetops of Tasmania for more than a year in protest of illegal logging. Your passion may not matter to anyone else, but if it matters to you, don't ignore it.

Every day matters. The awareness of our mortality can help us pursue a goal. We all have a limited amount of time on earth. Those who live in active awareness of this reality are more likely to identify goals and make progress toward them. Or to put it another way: Everyone dies, but not everyone truly lives.

Not everyone needs to believe in your dream, but you do. The support and understanding of others will vary. It doesn't matter what anyone else thinks about your quest, but if you don't have sufficient motivation to see it through, it will be tough going.

Before beginning a quest, count the cost. In the early days of my journey to every country, someone criticized it by saying all it required was a certain amount of time and money. I later realized that this perspective could actually be helpful. If I clearly understood exactly what was involved in "going everywhere," and if I then began working on each part of the goal step-by-step, it no longer seemed overwhelming. Whatever you choose to do, count the cost as much as you can.

We are motivated by progress and achievement. It feels good to check things off. Lists are both fun and motivational. We enjoy breaking things down step-by-step and incrementally conquering big challenges.

We can't always opt out of monotony, but we can choose which form it takes. Odysseus fought off sea monsters and escaped from an island prison, but he also endured a lot of boring days at sea. Most quests consist of a set of milestones that take a long time to reach. To stay on track, choose forward motion—keep making choices that bring you closer to the goal, even if it seems like reaching the end will take forever.

The effort is the reward. If you measure success by the opinions of others, you've effectively set yourself up for failure. But if you measure success by your own effort, focusing on what you produce and contribute, any additional praise or fame will be a bonus. The work itself can serve as its own motivation.

Some adventures should be shared. Tom Allen said that "a dream can have only one owner." But some challenges can be conquered jointly, and even if your quest isn't a tag team effort, chances are that a number of people will participate in your dream as you move toward completion.

Misadventures produce confidence. Getting stuck, detained, shut out, or set back is never fun, but these experiences are a necessary part of the journey. When something goes wrong, strive to accept it as an investment in learning. Hopefully, you won't make the same mistake twice . . . or at least, not over and over.

As you make progress toward a small goal, the bigger vision expands. Many people featured in the book started with a small goal that grew in scope as it became more feasible. If at first you can't picture a tremendous accomplishment, start with an achievable one. (Conversely, when you work toward a tremendous accomplishment, watch out: The next one may be even bigger.)

Quests do not always tie up well. Sometimes the ending is glorious, and sometimes it's bittersweet. Either way, take the time to process all you've been through. When you're ready, choose a new adventure.

Appendix 2

Cast of Characters

Name	Quest	Category	Status
Tom Allen	Bicycle around the world	Athletic	Restructured
Marc Ankenbauer	Jump in every lake in two of the largest U.S. and Canadian national parks (168 lakes in total)	Athletic	Completed
Izzy Arkin	Master karate in Kyoto, Japan, as the first step to becoming a ninja	Athletic	Completed
Ron Avitzur and Greg Robbins	Sneak into work at Apple for months to create software that later shipped on every computer	Creative	Completed
Elise Blaha	Create a life oriented around "serial crafting" projects	Creative	Completed
Mark Boyle	Travel from the United Kingdom to India without money	Activism	Restructured

NAME	QUEST	CATEGORY	STATUS
Nate Damm	Walk across the United States	Exploration	Completed
Rasanath Dasa	Leave Wall Street to live in a monastery in Manhattan	Self-discovery	Completed
Laura Dekker	Circumnavigate the world's oceans on a 38-foot sailboat as the world's youngest solo sailor	Exploration	Completed
Robyn Devine	Knit or crochet 10,000 handmade hats	Creative	In progress
Tina Roth Eisenberg	Publish a body of work promoting innovative design	Creative	In progress
Travis Eneix	Commit to a radical focus on his health and write down everything he ate for 1,000 days	Self-discovery	Completed
Nicholas Felton	Document life through an extensive series of personal annual reports	Documentation	In progress

NAME	QUEST	CATEGORY	STATUS
John Francis	Abstain from motorized transport and maintain a vow of silence for 17 years	Activism	Completed
Miranda Gibson	Protest illegal logging by climbing a tree in Tasmania and living there for more than a year	Activism	Completed
Seth Godin	Challenge the status quo by publishing a continual stream of ideas	Documentation	In progress
Kristen Goldberg	Complete the life list she first created when she was 16 years old—no modifications permitted	Self-discovery	In progress
Scott Harrison	Establish water charity, with the goal of giving access to clean water to every person in the world	Activism	In progress
Thomas Hawk	Take, edit, and publish one million photos	Documentation	In progress

NAME	QUEST	CATEGORY	STATUS
Meghan Hicks	Run the Marathon des Sables	Athletic	Completed
Josh Jackson	Attend a game at every Major League Baseball stadium	Exploration	In progress
A. J. Jacobs	Read the entire *Encyclopedia Britannica* in one year	Academic	Completed
Jia Jiang	Practice "Rejection Therapy" for 100 days and post the results on YouTube	Self-discovery	Completed
Julie Johnson	Train her own guide dog	Independence	Completed
Steve Kamb	"Level up" his life on an "Epic Quest of Awesome"	Self-discovery	In progress
Stephen Kellogg	"Climb the right ladder" by pursuing a career as an independent musician	Documentation	Completed
Juno Kim	Leave behind a traditional life in South Korea and become an advocate for female Asian travelers	Self-discovery	Completed

NAME	QUEST	CATEGORY	STATUS
Rita J. King	Create Science House and a series of "mystery jars"	Academic	Completed
Steven Kirsch	Find a cure for a rare blood disorder	Activism	In progress
Matt Krause	Walk across Turkey, ending at the Iranian border	Exploration	Completed
Isabelle Leibler	Train an untrainable horse	Athletic	Completed
Jay Leno	Master the art of stand-up comedy	Creative	In progress
Sasha Martin	Cook a meal from every country in the world	Creative	Completed
Mark McDonough	Capture the 1989 Rio Grande Heritage Unit train (among others) on camera	Documentation	Completed
Shannon O'Donnell	Travel through Southeast Asia with her 11-year-old niece	Exploration	Completed
Jiro Ono	Devote his life to mastering the preparation of sushi	Creative	Completed

NAME	QUEST	CATEGORY	STATUS
Alicia Ostarello	Go on 50 dates in all 50 states	Relational	Completed
Martin Parnell	Run 250 marathons in a single year (among other quests)	Athletic	Completed
Hannah Pasternak	Move to Israel and hike the National Trail	Exploration	Completed
Bryon Powell	Establish a community focused on ultrarunning	Athletic	Completed
Jerry Seinfeld	Master the art of stand-up comedy	Creative	In progress
Mani Sivasubramanian	Create a foundation that offers health-care access to low-income children in India	Activism	Completed
Phoebe Snetsinger	Set the world record for the most sighted birds	Exploration	Completed
Allie Terrell	Visit every basilica in the United States	Exploration	In progress
Gary Thorpe	Produce the world's largest symphony performance	Creative	Completed

Name	Quest	Category	Status
Helene Van Doninck	Become an advocate for non-lead ammunition	Activism	Completed
John and Nancy Vogel	Bicycle from Alaska to Patagonia with their twin 10-year-old sons	Exploration	Completed
John "Maddog" Wallace	Set the world record for running marathons in the most countries (100+)	Athletic	Completed
Adam Warner	Fulfill every goal on his late wife Meghan's life list	Self-discovery	In progress
Howard Weaver	Lead an epic battle to return Alaska's newspaper to the people of Alaska	Activism	Completed
Sandi Wheaton	Travel and photograph America's Route 66 after an unexpected layoff	Documentation	Completed
Gabriel Wyner	Become fluent in at least five languages to support his opera career	Academic	Completed

NAME	QUEST	CATEGORY	STATUS
Scott Young	Complete the 4-year MIT computer science curriculum in 1 year	Academic	Completed
Stephanie Zito	Give $10 every day to a different nonprofit organization for a year	Activism	Completed

Appendix 3

A Quest for Everyone

It's admirable to find one thing you love and make it your sole focus for a long period of time, just as many of the people in this book did. But if you're still not sure what that thing *is,* consider experimenting with smaller aspects of big goals.

Don't want to run one hundred marathons? Can't imagine running at all? No problem. Go out and *walk* twenty minutes.

Don't want to visit every country in the world? Great. Renew your passport and *go to one country* in the next six months.

Nineteen other ideas follow, all adapted from the quests in this book.

QUEST BAZAAR

BIG QUEST	WHO DID IT	BOOK PAGE	RELATABLE ALTERNATIVE
Move to Kyoto, Japan, to master karate and become a ninja	Izzy Arkin	46	Take a class in karate, taekwando, or other martial art.

Big Quest	Who Did It	Book Page	Relatable Alternative
Circumnavigate the globe on a solo voyage in a small sailboat	Laura Dekker	71	Go on a solo voyage of your own (small sailboat optional).
Practice tai chi and write down everything you eat and drink for 1,000 days	Travis Eneix	34	Log your daily activities for a week, paying attention to what you eat and how much you exercise.
Spend hundreds of hours documenting life to create a detailed personal annual report each year	Nicholas Felton	124	Spend a few hours on an annual review, in which you define priorities for your life and set goals for each year.
Take a vow of silence for 17 years	John Francis	42	Don't speak for a whole day.
Climb a tree to protest logging; remain there for 400 days	Miranda Gibson	184	Find something that bothers you, then find a small way to make it better for others.
Visit every country in the world	Chris Guillebeau		Visit a single new country.

Big Quest	Who Did It	Book Page	Relatable Alternative
Bring clean water to everyone in sub-Saharan Africa	Scott Harrison	41	Bring clean water to one village in Africa. Just $6,000 can sponsor an entire project that provides clean water, education, and follow-up visits. Visit charity water.org/donate.
Take, process, and edit one million photos	Thomas Hawk	64	Learn to improve the photos you take with your phone or hand-held camera. Commit to posting one a day for a year.
Read the entire *Encyclopedia Britannica* in one year	A. J. Jacobs	127	Read a different *Wikipedia* entry every day for a year.
Practice 100 days of "Rejection Therapy," visiting fire stations, restaurants, and other businesses with unusual requests	Jia Jiang	74	Practice a single experiment of Rejection Therapy. Ask for something unusual that you don't expect to receive. Pay attention to how you feel when making the request.

Big Quest	Who Did It	Book Page	Relatable Alternative
Become James Bond for a weekend as part of an "Epic Quest of Awesome"	Steve Kamb	129	Decide how to "level up your life" in your own way. Is there something you can learn, do, or become?
Walk across an entire country or continent	Matt Krause (and others)	9	Walk everywhere for a week, or at least a few days. Find creative ways to avoid motorized transport.
Cook a meal from every country	Sasha Martin	87	Broaden your culinary horizons—prepare a meal from a cuisine you haven't tried, or visit an ethnic restaurant you've never heard of.
Devote your life to making the best possible sushi	Jiro Ono	47	Visit a nice sushi restaurant and order "omakase style," where the chef determines your entire order based on the best ingredients of the day.

Big Quest	Who Did It	Book Page	Relatable Alternative
Visit every basilica in America to learn more about your faith	Allie Terrell	93	Visit a building of religious significance, either relating to your own faith or to a different one.
Become fluent in four or more languages to benefit an opera career	Gabriel Wyner	119	Learn to comfortably speak one foreign language. Everyone's a beginner at the beginning.
Complete the MIT computer science curriculum in one year	Scott Young	112	Enroll in a single online course (from MIT or elsewhere) and watch at least two of the lectures.
Give $10 every day to a different nonprofit for a year	Stephanie Zito	189	Give $100 to a new charity, then commit to learn more about it over the next year.

Index

About the Author

CHRIS GUILLEBEAU is an entrepreneur, a traveler, and a *New York Times* bestselling author. During a lifetime of self-employment that included a four-year commitment as a volunteer executive in West Africa, he visited every country in the world (193 in total) before his thirty-fifth birthday. For most of his adult life he has modeled the proven definition of an entrepreneur: "Someone who will work twenty-four hours a day for themselves to avoid working one hour a day for someone else."

Chris's first book, *The Art of Non-Conformity*, was translated into more than twenty languages. His second book, *The $100 Startup*, was an instant *New York Times* and *Wall Street Journal* bestseller with hundreds of thousands of copies sold worldwide.

Every summer in Portland, Oregon, Chris hosts the World Domination Summit, a gathering of creative, remarkable people. Connect with him on Twitter (@chrisguillebeau), write to him through his website, or say hi at your choice of international airline lounge.

ChrisGuillebeau.com
#FindtheQuest

Lead a Life of Adventure, Meaning, and Purpose—
and Earn a Good Living